The Art of Christian Living

The Art
of Christian Living

LAWRENCE M. McCAFFERTY

And the Word was made flesh,
and dwelt among us....

FOUNDED 1838

GPPS

G. P. Putnam's Sons   New York

Library of Congress Catalog Card
Number: 54-10498

MANUFACTURED IN THE UNITED STATES OF AMERICA

VAN REES PRESS • NEW YORK

TO MY FRIEND AND TEACHER

THE REVEREND DR. D. J. BUSSELL

Foreword

The author of *The Art of Christian Living* has written to make the world listen again to the great tenets of our faith and also he interprets Christianity anew for men of today. With quiet scholarship, with no attempt to provoke controversy or gain attention by any new or startling definitions of the essential steps along Christ's Way, he goes to the heart of the matter.

Simply yet in an engaging manner this book explains why Christianity is prayer and fasting, intelligence and understanding and many other things, but above all faith and love. It seeks to make of Jesus Christ something more than a myth or an historical figure. "We must cast aside all crutches and devices we have built up in our egocentric lives, all methods and techniques figured out by the intellect of man, all athleticism and will worship which passes for spiritual discipline." The author urges us instead to enter through the little door of faith and love into the Kingdom of God.

The successful delivery of such a message is a considerable achievement. I believe this to be a book of very great distinction in its field. It could, I think, with profit be added to the reference library of every theological seminary, whether Protestant or Catholic. Clergymen and educators and students generally will find it a source mine worth exploring. The style, too, is intriguing. I am indeed glad to recommend so fine a book—inspirational in the best sense—to the American public.

DANIEL A. POLING

Contents

Introduction

The forms and symbols of any culture are preserved in its arts and sciences which may be transmitted in various ways to successive generations. Each new generation must, however, approach these forms and symbols, and understand them in the way peculiar to that period. The plays of Shakespeare mean something far different to the person who reads them today from what they meant to one who read them in the age of Samuel Johnson. In each generation there are relatively few who succeed in mastering the traditional culture handed down to them. And these few, in turn, reflect an entirely different point of view from that of their predecessors who had access to the same forms.

In the historical perspective, the institution, which in its various phases, has been called Christianity, has been interpreted in each period of thought in the ways which were congenial to that age. Historians refer to the era of Scholasticism, the era of the Reformation, and the Modern Era. The basic doctrines of Christianity have been interpreted in the light in which each age has come to see them.

In turn, the "periods" of history have received their cast of thought from outstanding thinkers; so that one can point to Augustine or Aquinas, and Luther or Calvin, and immediately a certain period is called to mind.

It was Hegel who thought he could place the entire history of Christianity into a developmental scheme fitted to his philosophical theories. And his influence has been very extensive, even till this time.

Our age has come to think of history, including the history of Christianity, in terms of abstract generalizations and outstanding personalities who become billboards on which we post various labels and bits of information.

The purpose of this work is to draw attention to the fact that the religion of our Lord Jesus Christ cannot be fitted into any neat little scheme worked out by historians and held up for inspection to the reading public.

Christianity is Christ; and Christ is Life; and Life is the Spirit; and the Spirit is apprehended only by living men and women, individual souls, who realize their need of salvation from a condition of fear and a bondage to the confusion of values in a world that is lost in confusion and fear and dread. Behind the urbanity and the sophistication of the modern city-dweller moves a spirit of fear and uncertainty as the people of this age proceed closer to Eternity not knowing *why* or *how*.

The forms and symbols preserved in creeds and scriptures and confessions are little more than mere words until we awake to the fact that God has, in Christ, offered us a gift which is infinite in value. Again, we shall never know the meaning of this gift until we awake to the fact that God has given His Spirit through the Church to each individual who is willing to accept it—then move on to accept the Spirit and allow the light that it brings to show us that the Word which was made flesh is the same Word which speaks to us now through the Church (which is truly invisible) and opens the way to Eternal Life.

In the light of the above, it is evident that Christianity can never be made the subject of scholarly research and historical study. Knowing more about the Jesus of history, even if that were possible, will not bring us one step closer to Jesus as *He is now*.

This book suggests an alternative way to the study of Christianity, a way which will become evident to each person as he proceeds with the reading. It is addressed to those who want to know more than a mere rehash of information already available in well-documented studies. It will interest only those to whom Jesus Christ is more than a myth or an historical figure.

The Art of Christian Living

I

The Way to the Living God

CHRISTIANITY is neither the religion of the masses nor the religion of the intellectuals. It is the religion of each individual who stands in need of salvation and who has accepted our Lord and Savior Jesus Christ, who came into the world to save sinners. Jesus was neither a Marxist nor an intellectualist. As a man (for He was also a man), he spoke simply and directly to every man and woman who would hear him. In so doing, he established the pattern for everyone who would follow in his way. This way was a simple way, without complexity, so that *every* man might find the light of life who chose to accept the truth of existence, that is God.

But men have not been satisfied with the direct way to the Kingdom of God. They prefer to talk about the truth, to construct complicated theories which can be understood only by the one who has the patience to master all the technical terms which form a part of the complex. Those who differ with these intellectualists are shouted down as naïve—simply because they prefer Christ to words about Christ.

Jesus Christ was and is the Living Truth. One cannot come to Him by any other way than by the Way of Life. This state-

3

ment is of course a simple assertion. It has ample support in Scripture. But here it is of no use to summon texts to justify one's position. There are certain things which are clear and evident to one's senses—the fact that one breathes, walks, eats, sleeps, and so forth—that no one considers it necessary to prove. The Way of Life which *is* Christ stands in relation to the knowledge-process somewhat as our natural organic existence is related to the process of knowing. The Way is apprehended directly, immediately, without reference to concepts and ratiocination. It is obvious to the one *who is awake* and therefore able to know it. In sleep, we do not know our natural existence in a conscious manner. In the sleep of sin, we do not know our spiritual existence in a conscious way. But with the awakening of the spirit, the fact of Christ and the Way of Life become quite obvious. No amount of verbalization can alter or change the prime facts of existence on any "level." Facts exist for those who are awake to them. They are chimeras to the unawakened. So it is with the Spirit which is Christ. One is awake to Christ or one sleeps in sin. There is no other possibility. On the level of prime facts, there is always the *either/or*. It is the dilemma of some intellectuals to entertain the notion that relativity is a "universal law." But life and death are not relative. One either *is* or one is not. Either one has identity or one has not.

There are degrees of realization and appreciation of life and identity. But there is a point where these begin. For the Christian, that point is the creation of the individual soul by God, the Creator of all.

When, then, does real life begin for the individual who is to himself only a name, defined by a cultural heritage, a biological structure, a family, a physical environment? Before this question can be answered, it is necessary to see that the biological-complex-with-a-name is unconscious, that is he does not know what he really is. But he has a name. And perhaps in this fact lies a much deeper significance than the casual observer is wont to recognize. To call by name is often sufficient to arouse a person from slumber. We respond to another when we are called by name in a more immediate way, a more spontaneous way, than when we are addressed only in a general way.

A man is called by name only by those who know him, by those who are in some manner associated with him. Now Christ calls every man by name until he stirs in his sleep and is aroused by the summons. The Word calls us by name and our answer is the awakening to life. The Word is life and we are quickened by it. The Word is that boundless Identity who seals us with His identity so that when He speaks our name and we hear what we are called, we begin to live as conscious beings, responsive to Reality.

What, then, of that name we have received on earth? It was only a sound, a combination of letters to those who did not understand. But when *He* calls us by name, there is meaning and consciousness and life contained in the utterance. And those who hear, awake to life and consciousness and understanding. "Be still, and know that I am God" (Psa. 46:10).

In thinking upon and contemplating the way, the truth, and the life of our Lord and Savior, words form themselves gently and simply and clearly within the heart. It does not occur to one to ponder tediously how to phrase a thought so that the effect of learning, erudition, and intellect can be conveyed to the reader. When we think and write in the Presence of God it is impossible to consider how to be clever and obscure.

No, Christianity, as men call that which professes the Word of God, is not for any special group apart from the

5

whole of mankind. And since Christ Jesus came for all men, regardless of their station in this world, it is only fitting that we should speak and write so that all men may have access to the truth. For the wisdom which is of God lends not itself to the philosophies conceived by men who take lightly the Word of truth.

Howbeit we speak wisdom among them that are perfect: yet not the wisdom of this world, nor of the princes of this world that come to nought:

But we speak the wisdom of God in a mystery, *even* the hidden *wisdom,* which God ordained before the world unto our glory:

Which none of the princes of this world knew: for had they known *it,* they would not have crucified the Lord of glory.

But as it is written, eye hath not seen, nor ear heard, neither have entered into the heart of man, the things which God hath prepared for them that love him.

But God hath revealed *them* unto us by the Spirit: for the Spirit searcheth all things, yea, the deep things of God.

For what man knoweth the things of a man, save the spirit of man which is in him? even so the things of God knoweth no man, but the Spirit of God.

Now we have received, not the spirit of the world, but the spirit which is of God; that we might know the things that are freely given to us of God.

Which things also we speak, not in the words which man's wisdom teacheth, but which the Holy Ghost teacheth; comparing spiritual things with spiritual.

But the natural man receiveth not the things of the Spirit of God: for they are foolishness unto him; neither can he know *them,* because they are spiritually discerned.... For who hath known the mind of the Lord, that he may instruct him? But we have the mind of Christ. (I Cor. 2:6-14, 16)

There is nothing esoteric or mysterious about the Word of God. But one must be *in* the Word in order to know the

Word. William James' *The Varieties of Religious Experience* will not give us the keys to the Kingdom. But the Prayer of our Lord will.

There is no compromise possible between the Kingdom of God and the kingdom of man. But until men learn humility they cannot know what this lack of compromise means. When the lesson of humility has been learned, then men are called to go up to "a higher place."

In their anxiety to preserve the forms of worship and the symbols of a particular confession, many have sought by force, stratagem, or intellectual subtlety to impose a uniform observance upon all who seek to be Christians. Certainly we do not find this externalism and forceful imposition expressed in the attitude of Jesus as preserved in the Gospel records. Love inspires by its example and wins by its beauty. The soul that has looked into its depths and perceived the nothingness of the creature, the soul that has looked up and seen the all-ness of God—such a soul knows from experience the infinitude of love which streamed into the heart of man from Calvary, raising the soul to new life through the indwelling of the triune God.

Christ lives now in the heart of each man and woman who accepts him. For His life is an eternal present; and, when He lifts us up to share in His beatitude, we have already a beginning of eternal life as the moments of our lives are transformed into an eternal Now. We must have courage and work diligently for His Kingdom, but we labor in vain if it is not Christ who labors in us through His Kingdom already present in the hearts of those who love Him.

The myth of the nineteenth century, that progress is inevitable and automatic, is an exploded shibboleth alive only in the minds of those who do not know their own depths.

If there is more love, more light and more understanding in the world today, it is only because the Spirit of God has penetrated some lives more intensely and pervasively than in the past. If it seems darker in some quarters than ever before, it is simply because men have ignored the Gospel and allowed their souls to be taken captive by darkness and fear and hate.

It was part of the Reformation to break the crystallized molds of authoritarian religion with its hold over the lives of the laity through the ecclesiastical system. This part of the Reform was successfully carried out only to be succeeded by intellectual crystallization as soon as the new movement lost faith in the Divine Providence and sought to impose a system of rigid subordination to the letter as interpreted by the most popular theologians. It is then that one finds the Protestant world torn apart by infralapsarian versus supralapsarian doctrines of the Fall and by governmental versus judicial theories of the Atonement, among other things. This is neither the time nor the occasion to speculate about the possible alternatives available to the Reform parties especially during the first part of the seventeenth century. All we need to realize is that a most barren and sterile period followed the epoch of the religious wars. It was a period of intellectual and moral decline for the dominant parties of the Reform.[1]

Having realized the futility of Scholasticism, some of the theologians of the early nineteenth century—such as Schleiermacher and Ritschl—sought to reconstruct the principles of the Christian faith upon a foundation of the psychological structure of man. But, as Kierkegaard realized, God is not to be found in intellectual constructs nor is He to be found in

[1] See Maximin Piette, *John Wesley in the Evolution of Protestantism* (New York, Sheed and Ward, 1937).

8

the subjectivity of the individual. For He is neither an object which can be talked about, nor the subjective processes of the ego, nor the unconscious of psychology. He is to be found in the very center of our being. Nor could we exist if He were not present in us. We find God through prayer; that is, we commune with God when we have laid aside our ideas and feelings about Him and allowed Him to *be* in us. For that is essentially the meaning of faith: the casting aside of the ideas we have about God and the acceptance of Him as He is. Then He surely will reveal Himself to the eye of faith.

We are not speaking here of the methods of cloistered mysticism. Although ever since the Desert Fathers ran away from civilization to worship God in the wilderness, men have practiced and written about those exercises and ascetic practices which are supposed to prepare the soul for God. The unfortunate result of this separation of the religious from the secular has caused more misunderstanding and tragedy for civilization than perhaps any other single historical fact. The life of prayer is a continuous attitude which can and must be acquired and maintained by every member of a society composed of true Christians. The withdrawal from society of those who are deeply concerned with the life of prayer was and is a serious loss. For men of prayer are the spiritual fountains of civilization. Without their presence in our midst, decline and crystallization are inevitable. They are the *eyes* of civilization.

Credo ut intelligam.

Does this mean that we blindly accept with credulity or with the naïveté of an imbecile in order that we may intellectualize about the truths of faith? I hardly think so. Perhaps it meant this in decadent Scholasticism, either Catholic or

9

Protestant. But it certainly did not mean this for Augustine, Calvin, or Luther. And if not for these men, then how much *less* for those immediate followers and especially the disciples of Jesus? Not that we may assume that those who knew Jesus personally understood His teaching more than those who knew Him only by faith. "Blessed *are* they that have not seen, and *yet* have believed" (John 20:29). For there were those who knew Jesus personally who did not believe. Even followers such as Cleopas did not believe or they could not have spoken as they did about Christ, on the road to Emmaus. Contrary to the Liberal "Back-to-Jesus" Movement which assumed that if we knew more about the sources and the actual life that we would understand better— we find, from what records we have, that physical contact did not make for understanding. Only those who *believed*, understood. This was true then and will always be true. For this is the way to God.

I believe, in order to understand.

What, then, is this belief upon which so much depends? It is the *capacity* to receive the understanding. And what is the understanding? It is the knowledge of God, the Spirit of Truth, which makes us *be* and *do* what belief and faith make possible to us. And we know God who is love by the love which is born in us, which is the reason Saint Paul refers to charity (agape) as the bond of perfection—the making complete, the love which fulfills the Law and the prophets.

Saint Augustine exclaims, "O God, command what thou wilt and give what thou wilt command!" In this statement as in many other paradoxical statements made by the bishop of Hippo, we have an affirmation of faith which must be deeply understood in the light revealed by faith. For unless we walk by the light which is given through faith, we shall not walk at all. In faith, there is no accommodation to the "natural" man. We are lifted up that we may see what it is that we are made for and we are plunged into the depths that we may know it is God who both worketh and willeth in us the things which He commands.

How are we to know the things which are of Christ? Not by logical demonstration. But by the affirmation of His will which is that we love Him with our whole will, mind, soul, heart, and strength. He commands; but He also gives what He commands. The wisdom of God is foolishness unto man but it is no longer foolishness when we comprehend with all the saints what is the length and breadth and height and depths of the love of God. The mystery of paradox is solved, not by a blind leap of faith, but by a faith informed with love.

The witness of the Spirit has always been in the Church. It always will be. For God continually raises up souls to testify, not only by their words but by their lives, to the truth which is in Christ Jesus, our Lord. There is a witness of the Spirit to which each man is called. Blessed is the man who hears that call and responds!

The Reformation brought about vast changes. We need to understand these changes. For they have deeply influenced the life of everyone, whether he be Protestant or Catholic or nonsectarian. The research of many scholars gives us a many-sided interpretation of what actually took place, what the intention of the Reformers was, and what the effects have been since the sixteenth century. We will not find a uniform interpretation of all questions. But there is a body of agreement on certain basic aspects of the problem.

It can safely be said that their intention, basically, was to purify the Church.

Now in these latter days, we find many religious organizations which claim to be *the* Church. They pride themselves on being the adherents of some theological interpretation. Others pride themselves on having no theology or creed. But what earnest and thoughtful church member would honestly say that he believes his salvation depends upon the mere assent to a creed or a dogma?

The sixteenth century reformers formulated certain theological positions which the religious organizations adhering to these systems have accepted as standards of orthodoxy. However the Reformers themselves and their followers have maintained that they were restoring the purity of the Gospel as the way of salvation to all who believe. They did not consider themselves as innovators. Neither did they believe they were the first true Christians since apostolic times. Yet in the heat of theological debate things were said which would almost lead the observer to this conclusion. And it is these unfortunate divisions, based more often on appearance than on solid foundation, which have led to the abyss of separatism.

To purify the Church meant to return to the principles of Augustinianism. But whereas Augustine found his freedom in the advocacy of an established institution, the Reformers stressed the invisible church and found their freedom in championing a high spiritual conception of the Church.

But in stressing certain aspects of Augustine, his theology apart from his intense spirit of prayer, they tended to prepare the ground for theologism and intellectualism. To purify the Church means to separate the accretions, namely the things which are of man from the things which are of God. This purification is essentially very simple; in fact it is the spirit of simplicity, *sacred simplicity*, which purifies the Church. It is we who have made complexity. It is *de rigueur* to be complicated. It is the easiest way to pass as an authority among men if you can verbalize nonsense to the point of intellectuality. But as the followers of Korzybski would say, one is just making noises about noise.

We cannot even talk about purifying the Church. God has created the Church; He maintains it and He will bring it into glory. For the Church is everlasting.

Men have tried to convince themselves that the religious organizations they have constructed are the true Church. But that is superstition—placing intellectually constructed ideas over the real creation of God.

Calvin was right when he said that the true Church is invisible. He was also right when he said that only the elect are members of the true Church. Yet anyone who wills *is* of the elect. This is, of course, a paradox with which the intellect will never be satisfied. But we have been given the spirit of truth so we may understand the things which are of God.

It is good that Protestants should seek reunion. But what is the basis for such action? Surely it can some about only as the sects transcend their differences by ceasing to be Protestant or Catholic and by becoming truly Christian. Now this is precisely what the Reformation aimed to achieve. But as soon as the formulas became more important than the end for which they were framed, just that soon did the Reformation fail. And certainly the history of the latter part of the seventeenth and eighteenth centuries is a history of the failure of the great intent of the Reformation. The rationalism of that period could not have been so destructive otherwise.

We must find the spirit of Christianity, which means that we must seek the spirit of Christ who is even now the Lord and Master of all those who have believed in order to understand.

More important than any system, the Reformation bequeathed to us the liberty of turning to the Bible and finding therein the Word of God. The exultation of this liberty released men from bondage to the past. Yet we must not forget, as many have seemed to forget in new-found enthusiasm, that the Word had been witnessed to in each age, that the Church is found wherever truly Christian souls are found. And these two facts have been with us always. Hence we are brought once again to the conclusion that the Church of God is not equatable with any religious organization. It is invisible and is composed of the elect in every age. Still we do not minimize the importance of ecclesiastical organization, indispensable to man in the state of civilization; for in it he realizes fellowship in actualizing his potentialities.

The concept of perfecton is not new with Christianity. We find traces of it in our earliest literature in the West and also in the East. But the more exact usage it received in the hands of the Greeks in the term, τέλειος, rendered its meaning more precise and therefore more understandable and usable. This is the form in which it occurs in the New Testament. It denotes wholeness, completeness, fulfillment. It suggests the end or fulfillment, the term or goal of any living process in the scale of entities and beings. (It is the seed fulfilled in the tree.)

All of these ideas, when employed in a naturalistic way, can be conceived only in terms of process or change—the passage from one stage of development to another which more nearly approaches the goal of the organism. By observation one can make all these deductions and many others. And by studying the life cycle of a butterfly it is possible by induction to develop some concept of transformation which can be applied to many "levels" of life.

In the natural sphere—and the Greeks made their greatest

contribution in the natural order—the levels of causation defined by Aristotle are simply abstractions drawn from an observation of the way the existential unity behaves in its natural environment. The application of Greek, especially Aristotelian categories, results in clear and precise concepts which efficiently describe the process from the *terminus a quo* to the *terminus ad quem* in the life cycle of an organism. It must be remembered that Aristotle made a concentrated study in the biological sphere and arrived at his famous categories of causation by a process of induction. He cannot, therefore, be bracketed with the Cartesian rationalists of the "Enlightenment," as is so commonly done. In life we do not find that a person is either a suckling or an adult. The suckling is an adult in *potentiality*. Descartes and his English disciple, Locke, failed to comprehend this important distinction between the logic of life and the logic of abstractions; we find, by extension, that they fell into the absurd premise that a person is either a child or an adult by the simple fact that they made a universal application of the mathematical principle of the law of noncontradiction. The result was the billiard ball universe of David Hume, a lot of little substances floating about in space with no apparent connection or "chain of causation." Now the perfection of which Christ speaks is not the perfection of the natural order. Not that He denied the natural sphere, the realm of natural processes of unfoldment. His parables make use of the imagery derived from nature. But the precept Christ gave us was to be perfect *as our Father in heaven is perfect*. The difference is in *kind*. Jesus was always calling this distinction to the attention of His followers. The perfection of which Christ speaks comes from *above*. And that "above" is also within us and about us, not literally, but in *reality*. For the

Kingdom of heaven cometh not with observation. The Kingdom of heaven is within.

God is not an entity with numerically divisible parts. The allness of God and the simplicity of God are identical. He is not a Being limited by "dimensions," a term which is now recognized as being entirely relative. He is not a substance like one of Hume's billiard balls floating in space. At this point it would be possible to begin a discourse on Dionysian superlatives to describe the indescribable. Or one could borrow the terminology of the new physics to explain the relativity, for example, the finiteness of dimensional existence. But these things have been well done already and the modern, informed reader has immediate access to scientific and philosophical treatises. Of greater significance is the fact that verbal "descriptions" of the dimensionless are not only impossible but highly misleading. For the person is led to believe that because the terms *infinite, boundless, omnipotent, reality,* and so forth, have become theoretically intelligible to him, he therefore is in possession of their content. Nothing could be further from the truth. The philosopher who knows that God is infinite is no nearer to understanding God than is the child who knows that God is his real Father. He may be further away. If a man would know the simplicity of God, let him become simple. Let him be free from verbalisms; and, without denying the value of abstractions in their place, let him be free from words as a means of knowing God. Let him seek rather with his heart and soul and mind and will. And God will show him who and what He is.

There are unfortunately too many persons who have not learned, or who have forgotten, how to distinguish between a paradox and a confused thought. The result is not increased depth of comprehension but more muddleheadedness that passes for wisdom. *Wisdom is mine, saith the Lord!* It has always been and it always will be. Christians ought rather to ask God for wisdom than to devise clever means for obscuring their own ignorance.

Perfection then is the gift of God. As James wrote, "Every good gift and every perfect gift is from above, and cometh down from the Father of lights, with whom is no variableness, neither shadow of turning" (James 1:17). God has given man an intelligence which is able to think and meditate upon and receive the Word of God. It is the mentality of man which distinguishes him from the other members of the animal kingdom. The Bible teaches us that man in his nature is the image (symbol) and likeness of God. Now if man bears in his being the impress of God, it is certainly not obvious. And this is because men have *forgotten* their true nature, which is to be and express the semblance, the idea, of God. In theological parlance this falling away is termed the Fall of man.

The so-called modern period of history has a very narrow concept of the mind of man and a thoroughly confused notion about the *imago dei*.

Before we can proceed further to an understanding about the meaning of perfection as the goal of Christian life, we must clarify the basic concept of man as the created image of God.

For the examination of the parts of the term *perfection* clearly indicates that there is a way, a process, by which perfection comes into our lives. For the fact is, we are not perfect as we find ourselves in this material existence.

Once we have accepted the fact that there is an end, a goal, for mankind beyond the physical expression (as all Christians do accept and as reason when intelligently applied would suggest), it is a very simple matter, then, to examine the means at man's disposal for the attainment of that end. For unless there be an end, there can be no means. There can be only a conglomeration of facts which point nowhere. But once we *accept* the fact that there is an end, even though we may not clearly comprehend that end, we place ourselves in a position to appreciate it and gradually to apprehend it through the light of meaning which then illuminates the way. For the way to perfection is inseparably connected with the goal. Otherwise there could be no way. No one has ever conceived of a road that led nowhere. A city cannot be conceived without an access to it and an outlet from it. For all things are connected one with another. And there is nothing in this universe which is not related to everything else. Our failure to see this simple fact is a good indication of just how blind we are in our self-enclosed darkness.

We must open ourselves to the goal and let it come to us. Does this sound strange and paradoxical? Let us not be deceived by words. The end, the goal, is perfection. God is perfection, and perfection is love—the law fulfilled—*now, eternally now.*

It is important at the very outset clearly to understand the function of language and its place with respect to the subject at hand or, for that matter, to any subject. The discussion may seem elementary. It may seem an affront to the reader's intelligence. But modern research into the science of semantics, and into its more specialized branch "general semantics," indicates the need for more care in this direction than has been heretofore practiced. An accurate design projects on a plane of two dimensions the appearance of a structure in three dimensions. All the integral factors must be included in exact proportion and relation to each other in terms of the required perspective. No one would identify the design with the project. But many persons identify words with the object. The complexity multiplies the moment we shift attention to a verbal description. How greatly increased are the possibilities of error caused by our being conditioned to the words we all use in common, so that no two people have the same shade of meaning for any word that they use. Yet language is our means of communication in society. When we compare "objects" in the physical world and apply to them the terms evolved with the growth of language, our physical senses corroborate our impressions. We are able to compare shape and contour and the other aspects of form and color; and, by use of the mental processes, we are able to organize a frame of reference sufficiently intelligent to enable us to exist in a relative world.

But when we come to the language of Scripture we are confronted with facts which need only to be stated for one immediately to sense, if not to perceive, what a vast partition separates the natural from the divine realm. What are we to do with, how are we to understand such a saying as, "The words that I speak unto you, *they* are spirit, and *they* are life" (John 6:63)? We might be left in a quandary were it not for the statement immediately preceding, "It is the spirit that quickeneth; the flesh profiteth nothing." Obviously the Divine Master was speaking of the tongue which uttered the words and the wave lengths of sound which carried the phonetics of a now dead language when He referred to the flesh. And the words which He termed *life* and *spirit* were the Reality to which the spoken expression bore witness.

Yet the Master assures those who receive Him that they can approach the Father who is in secret, that is, who is separated from all that can be observed. "No man hath seen

God at any time" (John 1:18). It is in this sense that God is "wholly other." But He is not inaccessible as some maintain who have not yet understood.

Between the natural world, which can be observed and studied with all the precision which the physical sciences have developed, and the world of Spirit, which no man can penetrate as man, there is the vast and shadowy realm of the psyche. Those who have not made themselves acquainted with the religious literature of the past have come to assume that the psyche was a largely unexplored realm until the advent of Freud and Watson. Nothing could be further from the facts. Labels have changed but not the content for which they stand. Allowing for some variation because of racial, cultural, geographic elements (among others), the fact remains that the basic structure of the human psyche has had a continuity of identity through a cycle of time vaster than we have been able to record in the known annals of civilization.

Certain facts which formerly were gained through purely introspective and intuitive means have now been made the subject of study in a clinical environment where methods borrowed from the physical sciences are now applied, with modifications, to the elements of psychical research. Jung's "collective unconscious" and Rhine's "extrasensory perception" are gradually acquiring respectability in an age obsessed with physical observation; and, among other discoveries, these findings are establishing the fact that man is so united interiorly by links which bind him to the past and also to his contemporaries the world over that he is now in a better position to evaluate that which his ancestors understood in simpler and more direct ways. (That is, the pre-Cartesian ancestors.) Yes, it would seem that the "billiard ball" universe has gone the way of a retreating group of shibboleths which have obscured from the modern generations the truth of man's existence.

Modern physics, especially, has shown us that we are no longer living in a world of isolated units of substance called matter. The "solid" universe including man is recognized as an appearance. The infinitesimal particles which compose the body are termed *configurations of energy,* and space reigns supreme. Our bodies are porous to the waves of light that fill a space which has existence but no dimension. As distance is contingent upon at least two objects in space, so time, as it is generally conceived, is contingent upon the duration or the interval between the genesis and the maturity of a thing. It is not necessary to consider the elaborate proofs for these findings. It is enough to know that both extension and duration are recognized to be relative in scope and significance.

We mention these simple facts because it may *help* some to realize that the universe is open to God, that His all-presence includes them, and that we are indeed the Temples of the living God.

Once we face these facts we realize that the only reason we are not conscious of God is that we do not accept Him. This may seem harsh to one who feels he has lived a moral life of good will and brotherly kindness. But we are speaking of God and man—"For in him we live, and move, and have our being" (Acts 17:28)—not of the relations *between* men alone.

We are living in a world far different from the one that our bodily senses present to us. Every educated person accepts this conclusion today quite as a matter of course. It is not a philosophical problem as it was to Kant. Most of us, however, do not stop to consider that the psyche is also a configuration of energy; that our thoughts and emotions grouped around a co-ordinating center, the ego, are energy impulses, moving in lines of force according to a definite pattern, one that is unique with each individual. Furthermore it is now recognized, accepted, and practiced in the new field of psychosomatic medicine that the mind and the body are a co-ordinated unit, each aspect affecting the other. We have thus a recognition on the part of science of the traditional Christian teaching of the unity of the mind and the body.

Tying together the threads of discussion so far enumerated and outlined, we have the picture of a universe which is literally a pattern of units of existence tending toward One in whom we live and move and have our being. O God! The beauty of Thy face is seen in all who turn their gaze toward Thee, Thou infinite splendor! Thy rays emitting love are found in every heart that holds Thy secret caringly! We are all one in Thee, O God! How infinite is Thy glory!

Herein lies the significance, the meaning, of the new view of the universe—that the Creation, although it presents many aspects to the senses, is yet one, a many-sided unity. We will miss the point entirely if we think of this One as a numerical abstraction. For infinite diversity obtains as well as infinite individuality. There is distinction without separation.

We live in an unfolding universe. That is, each organism unfolds its potentialities according to a certain *pattern* and *sequence*. But in the human kingdom there are possibilities that do not exist in the animal kingdom. For the animal is a *closed* unity; whereas the human being is an *open* unity. The animal potentiality is fixed and determined, but the human shows forth the *possibility* of becoming unconditioned. We underscore possibility; for man may also through wrong choice or *lack of choice* become even more conditioned than the animal, which at least moves in harmony with the life of its species through its conative endowments.

For those who can receive it, "Now are we the sons of God" (I John 3:2). And being sons, we dwell in the Kingdom, and being in the Kingdom we are one with the Father, thus fulfilling the prayer of Jesus "that they may be one, as we are" (John 17:11).

In a universe in which all the member units are undergoing transformation and change according to God's unfolding Plan, all are called through the mercy of His Son to participate in the freedom of God's realm. Nor need we step outside this sphere; for the realm of God is within and about us eternally. For in God there is no time, as we understand it, no sequence and duration; neither do we find any distance, extension or dimension in Him; for He is all in all. *And in His Son, He has ascended above all heavens that He might fill all things.*

When we find our place in Him, as we are invited to do, then we are in a position to understand how *all things work together for good* because then truly do we love God—when we are in Him who first loved us.

There are times when we see things in a natural way. Again there are times when we are lifted into the realm of the Lord of Glory. Then do we see indeed.

God has intended this blessing for us *now* if we will make ourselves ready by *allowing* ourselves to be transformed through the renewing of our minds. Then we shall be translated into the Kingdom of His dear Son. For now is the time of acceptance.

But man, through that which distinguishes him as man, —that is, his mind—is open in all directions. He can move in

23

any direction. He can give his attention to anything in his cosmic or microcosmic environment. Indeed, progress, which the nineteenth century worshiped in a rather blind way, is a category in the realm of man's existence which applies to any direction in which he may give his attention. Hence we can progress toward degeneration or toward regeneration. In fact, man is presented with precisely this alternative. For in not choosing, man has chosen not to choose, so he is responsible. And the fatalistic psychology which passes for wisdom in some circles is merely sophisticated ignorance.

The Son of God has come. He has preached the Gospel of the Kingdom. And, as has been promised in Revelation, *anyone who wills may drink of the waters of life freely*. Therefore he who rejects the gospel has rejected the realm of God and the hope of glory. The heart that opens in recognition of the fact of spiritual transformation comes to know a blessing which changes all things within the mind into images capable of reflecting the glory of God. The Son of God is Himself the promise of transfiguration, even as it was His experience.

The medievals developed and universally applied the ancient concept of *hierarchy*, a term employed by clerical thinkers. Aristotle is, of course, the inspiration for these neat divisions of creation into easily manipulated categories. It is a triumph of the intellect at the cost of the Spirit. The Spirit moves where it wills and no intellect, whether angelic or human, can divine the purposes of God. Yet all is of love, and here we are not dealing with a magnified human will. Even the Son of God made a distinction between His will and the Will of the Father.

The far-reaching effect of this use of the principle of hierarchy can be justly appreciated only by those who have been exposed to its influence in their own interior lives. For we are not dealing here solely with intellectual abstractions but with dynamic forces, the effects of which are very tangible to those who have been exposed to their influence. It is not necessary to practice the spiritual exercises of Ignatius of Loyola in order to understand. But it is necessary to penetrate the form of the dogma to sense its dynamics, the way it works upon the psyche. For rigid dogmas are simply the crystallized psychic experience of innumerable adherents to the dogmatic structure.

Protestants who are not used to dealing with the psyche, having given their attention to the intellectual side of dogma, may not be able to appreciate just exactly what we are encountering in that extraordinarily complex phenomenon, the Roman Catholic Church. But it is well for us to get acquainted with the basic facts to be able intelligently to cope with them.

The origin for this intellectual application of the principle of hierarchy is found in Plato's hierarchy of archetypes and Aristotle's hierarchy of causes. The origin of the political organization of the Roman Catholic Church is the Roman Empire, especially the organization of the provinces. The source of the hierarchical principle applied to angelic intelligences and to the spiritual life of man is found in the writings of Dionysius, the Pseudo-Areopagite and his followers. And through the Degrees of Humility and the Degrees of Love of Bernard of Clairvaux we find its application to the contemplative life as conceived by medieval asceticism. Bernard and Richard of Saint Victor transformed the Song of Solomon into an allegory of the spiritual quest. And it is essentially the piety of Saint Bernard that illuminates the theology of Aquinas. It may seem somewhat facile to indicate a few individuals and credit them with the founding and inspiration of vast influences. But this is not done with the intention of isolating these persons. Rather it must be remembered that each of these persons was bound up with his time in terms of its aspirations, moods, intellectual comprehension. Possibly the individual was in revolt against these times as Saint Bernard certainly was. But these individuals appear, through their literary remains, in the writings and religious dogmas of later generations of churchmen.

Under the influence of Bernard's example, the Song of Solomon was commented upon for several centuries by writers of Roman Catholic spirituality. Even so cosmopolitan a religious genius as Francis of Sales resorts to the imagery of the Canticle of Canticles to describe his experience of nearness to God. The writings of John of the Cross are filled with the sexual imagery of the Song of Songs in which the soul's relation to God is pictured in terms of the relation between the sexes.

The problem of the use of sexual imagery to describe the soul's relation to God has been profoundly misunderstood by Protestant intellectualists and moralists. Having suffered the effects of the puritan revolt in religion, Protestant religionists of the past pushed sex into a dark closet and drew a curtain over the closet door. This is neither to condemn nor to justify such a reaction. But it is only to point out that this attitude has not solved, but only complicated and obscured, the problem of the emotional life of Christians who seek a more intense awareness of the truth of their religion. The relegation of sex to the parlor of the psychoanalyst has resulted in the complete exclusion of God from an important aspect of life.

Christians outside the pale of Catholicism do not, as a rule, have much acquaintance with the psychic effects of meditation as it is employed in the Roman Catholic Church. A thorough treatment of this subject would require a very lengthy analysis which yet remains to be done. Reductionist studies have been made by James Henry Leuba and others, but they have not been helpful because of their distorted perspective.

Quite apart from the psychological aspect of this problem, which is of course in the realm of effects and not of spiritual causes, we must face the spiritual significance of this concept of the soul's relation to God for a vital spiritual religion, the way of life in action. This can best be brought out through contrast with the imagery used by Jesus and His disciples to describe the relation of the soul to God.

The first and basic point to be observed in the concept of the soul symbolized in the Song of Songs by the Shulamite, is that it emphasized the *eros principle*, the sense of longing and emotional craving for a desired object. The feminine passive role, which the individual soul is made to assume, automatically excludes the major emphasis of the Lord Jesus Christ, namely that we are called to be the *sons of God*, inheritors of the Kingdom of His Glory.

Catholic theology posits God as the sole reality. Creation has a *received* existence. It is fundamentally unsound to say, as many Protestants do, that Catholicism is a fusion of Greek rationalism and Roman legalism. This statement is altogether too glib and superficial. To begin with, the rational thinking of the Greeks was very different from that rationalism which is identified with the French and English deists of the seventeenth and eighteenth centuries.

"There is but one God and this God is Being, that is the corner-stone of all Christian philosophy, and it was not Plato,

27

it was not even Aristotle, it was Moses who put it in position." [2]

This highly significant statement receives its justification in the following citation.

It seems, then, to borrow an expression from William James, that the Christian mental universe is distinguished from the Greek mental universe, by ever more and more profound structural differences. On the one side we have a god defined by a perfection in the order of quality: Plato's Good; or by a perfection in one of the orders of being: Aristotle's Thought; on the other side stands the Christian God Who is first in the order of being, and Whose transcendence is such that, in the vigorous phrase of Duns Scotus, when we have a first mover of this kind it needs more of a metaphysician to prove that He is first than it does of a physicist to prove that He is a mover. On the Greek side stands a god who is doubtless the cause of all being, including its intelligibility, efficiency and finality—all, *save existence itself* [italics mine]; ... on the Christian side a universe which begins to be by a creation. On the Greek side, stands a universe contingent in the order of intelligibility or in the order of becoming; on the Christian side a universe contingent in the order of existence. On the Greek side, there is the immanent finality of an order interior to beings; on the Christian side the transcendent finality of a Providence who creates the very being of order along with that of the things ordered. [3]

In this time, the dominant note of which is confusion, it is extremely important that we get the right perspective especially in the ordering of concepts. For our actions are based upon our thoughts. And, as Buddha sagely observed, man becomes what he thinks.

[2] Etienne Gilson, *The Spirit of Mediaeval Philosophy* (New York, Charles Scribner's Sons, 1936), p. 51. Excerpts reprinted by permission.
[3] *Ibid.*, p. 81.

All things are comprehended in God as one simple unity. But all *things* are not God nor is God all things. The *being* of all things is God and without Him would not anything exist. In so far as anything exists, it exists *in* God but it is not God, for God cannot be anything. Neither can He be comprehended except by Himself.

For Plato, God is the supreme Good, the highest value. For Aristotle, God is the supreme Thought, the first cause of all contingent beings. But we do not find a God who is essence and existence itself. The first reference we have to such a God in the history of Christian thought is, possibly, that in the Hortatory epistle to the Greeks, circa the third century: "The *He who is* [ὁ ὄν] of the Hebrews is the *that which is* [τὸ ὄν] of the Greeks."

The doctrine of creation *ex nihilo,* which we find employed early by Origen, rightly emphasizes the fact that there is no *thing,* no *matter,* out of which God created the universe, as some anthropomorphic deity might be conceived to have done by literally taking clay and molding it into some tangible proportions.

All creation has been conceived and *given* existence, life and intelligence by God. Hence we find there is not analogy of *proportion* between the Creator and the created. But there is an analogy of being, which might be stated simply in such a proposition as *because God is, I am.* Herein is expressed the radical contingency of the created upon the Creator in the order of existence and essence. If we view the concept of the *imago dei* in the above light, we have an order free from the obscurity which the principle of hierarchy plunges all thought into when it is applied to metaphysics. All ancient and medieval thought was obsessed with the idea of hierarchy. One constantly reads of levels, degrees, stratifications, from the seven heavens to the seven degrees of prayer. We find in these ideas a basis common to all the older branches of the Church.

The transition from the symbolic mode of thinking to the rational method of demonstration (pre-Cartesian) was well in evidence by the time of Bernard of Clairvaux. By the time of Duns Scotus the symbolic, intuitive mode of apprehension was the accepted approach of a diminishing minority. An illustration of the tendency to identify knowledge with logical demonstration is the following citation from the prayer of Duns Scotus opening the *De primo rerum omnium principio:*

> O Lord our God, when Moses asked of thee as a most true Doctor, by what name he should name Thee to the people of Israel; knowing well what mortal understanding could conceive of Thee and unveiling to him Thy ever blessed name, Thou didst reply: *Ego sum qui sum;* wherefore art Thou true Being, total Being. *This I believe, but if it be in any wise possible this I would also know. Help me, O Lord, to seek out such knowledge of the true being that Thou art as may lie within the power of my natural reason, starting from that being which Thou Thyself hast attributed to Thyself.* [Italics added] [4]

Here we have a clear and fully stated concept which presents the antithesis of that approach to knowledge of God represented by Saint Augustine and, later, by Saint Bernard of Clairvaux, William of Saint-Thierry, and others down to this very day who have sought God where only He can be found by *man,* namely at the center of his being. No one can fail to be moved by Augustine's account of his search for God. For this is the statement of maturity when the natural

[4] The prayer of Duns Scotus is cited by Gilson, *op cit.,* pp. 51-52.

light of reason is superseded by that clear light in which "there is no darkness at all" (I John 1:5).

The only integral philosophy for Christianity is the one based on the principle *know thyself*. For the true state of man is *to be in the world, yet not of the world*. And it is only by coming to know who and what we really are that we can understand and fulfill this precept of our Master. We have to apply more than logic if we are to find truth. Any age which, like the age of Scholasticism and the eighteenth century, overvalues intellect (though in each case intellect has been given a very different interpretation, as the Neo-Thomists rightly say) as a means of gaining a knowledge of reality, can justly be termed *rationalistic*. It matters not the shape of the garment. It may further be added that this present time, though it has taken on the guise of mechanism, is equally rationalistic. And equally, any trust in a *theory* of anti-intellectualism is caught in the same web of causation though anti-intellectualism emerges as reaction.

Heresy has been well defined as the partial representation of the truth. But this statement must be viewed from all sides before its meaning becomes clear. We can state a basic truth, for example the importance of "hearing" the Word. A whole theology can be constructed on this one principle so that the entire truth is seen only in the light of one facet. The obvious result is exaggeration and an *unbalanced* presentation. A very familiar example is the political propaganda of the twentieth century. Some actual facts are treated in such a way that the end product is a lie. Principles can be rearranged so that distortion is the outcome. Crudely illustrated, the word LIVE is composed of the same letters as the word EVIL. The only thing wrong is that one word is spelled completely opposite to the other. Let not the sensitive mind be shocked by the childlike illustration. For the plain fact of the matter is that evil is the wrong arrangement, the disordering of the elements of truth.

In the world of art, poetry, and literature we have been witnessing a veritable orgy of delight in the twisting of the truth. Baudelaire's *Fleurs du Mal* is only a more popular example of a trend which has become the fashion. The writings of André Gide are a most clever and diabolical twisting of the truth. The most sacred principles of life are used to fashion a world of imagery that destroys the likeness of God in those who accept and become what these images suggest. Yet we "moderns" give these sinister corruptions of truth the highest literary awards. Those who object can hear the cynical question proposed by Pilate, "What is truth?" (John 18:38).

The Bible contains the Word of God. But we can give a minor place to the words of Jesus Christ and overstress the words attributed to Moses. The result would be the failure of "rightly dividing the word of truth" (II Tim. 2:15).

Jesus accused the Pharisees of neglecting the "weightier *matters* of the law" (Matt. 23:23), because they overstressed the details of ritual observance. In the twentieth century we find persons who believe that the message of the Gospel is primarily one of social reform—that Jesus was attempting to change the political and social structure, primarily, when He was stressing the principle of love.

Roman Catholics believe that the Church is the major instrument of salvation in the world, and by Church they mean the hierarchy of bishops and priests whom they believe to be carrying on the apostolic succession.

Since there have been so many distortions of the truth from the time of the Gnostic heresies down to the twentieth century, it is well to consider the true meaning of the Church and its major concern.

It is an interesting fact that Augustine, who did so much to establish the Roman interpretation of the Christian religion, also held the view that the true Church was invisible and spiritual—that the actual ecclesiastical organization was composed of both the saved and the lost.

The Church is not an organization of men. It is the Body of Christ, that is the *teaching* in its absolute purity. Wherever Christ is, there is the Church. The Church is the presence of Eternity in time. The Word of God speaks through the Church.

This truth raises the concept of the Church high above the level of politics and the confused interpretations of man-made theologies.

There are those who talk about the theology of the Reformation as though it were to be compared with the medieval constructions of the Scholastics. There is no basis in fact for this point of view. It is of course true that the post-Reformation theology tended to be concerned with matters which were more scholastic in nature. But the high Reformation concept *intended* to be an affirmation of the Word of God rather than a system constructed in the light of the natural reason.

The Word of God speaks through the Church. Calvin recognized this truth. He also knew that the true Church is invisible. In fact, it was this truth that made it possible for the Reformation to become established as a movement apart from the all-encircling Roman ecclesiastical body. The efficient structure erected by the men of Geneva, which later passed into the religious life of Western Europe and America, was intended to be a means for advancing the Word of God.

The doctrines which the early Calvinists chose to emphasize, such as the sovereignty of God, were exaggerated only by those men who possessed a disputatious spirit.

Augustine said that there has never been a time that the Christian religion did not exist. He recognized along with some of the apologists that men of old had been inspired by the Word to produce those things needful to a particular group of people. That which was revealed in part among earlier races for their edification was now fully manifest in Christ Jesus.

The men of the Reformation realized that the Word which was made flesh in Jesus must be received again in faith by those who would understand the Teaching. Those, then, who allow the Word to penetrate their hearts with true understanding, are the ones who place themselves in a position to be received into the Body of Christ, the Church of God. And the fruit of the heart which is converted by the Word of God is a life of righteousness and peace in the Holy Spirit.

Important as ecclesiastical organizations may be, and are, in the existence of socialized man, they cannot be confused with the Church. It is the responsibility of the ministry to make this distinction clear. But unfortunately the distinction is not held before the laity for their consideration and understanding. It is to be hoped that the Protestant denominations achieve the recognition of this basic fact of the unity of the Church and place it above the struggle for ecumenicity at the level of fellowship.

God does not need large and powerful organizations of men to effect His designs in the world. Of course this is not very flattering to the ego of man, which is always making schemes to improve upon the Providence of God. Religious organizations under the leadership of the ministers and elders should rather prepare their membership to hear and receive the Word that it may prove fruitful in a life of righteousness and service to God and man.

The salvation of souls and the growth in grace under the inspiration of the Word of God must be the major concern of the organized groups of Christians throughout the world. Not only preaching but the direction of souls (the care of souls) must occupy a large part of the attention of the clergy. This last aspect of the ministry has been much neglected by Protestants, and unfortunately the need for guidance and counsel in the life of grace cannot be taken care of by a secular body of professional counselors and psychologists.

The great spiritual directors of the seventeenth century made it a cardinal point to allow the Holy Spirit to guide their direction of souls. And it is precisely this point which enabled them to act so wisely in their cures.

Under the stress of the times, the Reformers paid only a small amount of attention to the cure of souls as compared to their great concentration upon polemics and doctrinal questions. Too often the personal side of religion has been neglected for doctrine and allowed to degenerate into a maudlin sentimentality and emotionalism. This, I believe, is directly the result of long-standing neglect on the part of the clergy, which believed that its function and duty had been fulfilled when the sermon had been preached.

Prayer is the essence of Christianity. And prayer is simply the raising of the mind to God. "Thou wilt keep *him* in perfect peace *whose* mind *is* stayed *on thee*" (Isa. 26:3). Prayer is a special quality of attention which, when it is complete, allows only the Reality of God to exist in consciousness. Lips that move to form the words of prayer while the thought remains dull, heavy, and lifeless are mouthing the nothingness of sin.

When Jesus commanded the disciples—and through them, us—*to pray without ceasing,* he was referring to something much more basic than the repetition of words. He was speaking of attitude. In other words, he was admonishing us to remain in the attitude of prayer; that is, we must so think and live and express that we are at all times ready to commune with God in complete attention. We must be in the realm of God, namely in the place where God can be reached.

It matters not how much you know. But it is extremely important how you approach what you know.

The great problem of the intellectual mind in this period is, quite simply, confusion. Gone is the certainty of the medieval Scholastic; gone is the false clarity of the Age of Reason; gone even is the studied agnosticism and the bluff assurance of nineteenth century positivism and critical philosophy. Only among certain coteries in the academic world is there any clearly defined position. And these are being forced to modify their position under the constant pressure of new findings. While it is true that objectivity requires a suspension of judgment and a neutral attitude toward all new findings and hypotheses, it does not follow that decision and a positive exercise of faith are outmoded categories of action and expression. Everyone knows that the so-called scientific attitude toward objects that present themselves to attention began to take hold on a broad scale amongst the intelligentsia when Descartes put forward his attitude which can be epitomized by the words: "I doubt, in order to know."

Radical doubt, or nonacceptance, has its place in the area of appearances, the constantly changing pattern of formation and transformation. It is at best a highly limited method of obtaining knowledge.

Yet the intellectual mind has acquired the attitude of non-acceptance and doubt; and, true to the spirit of the original impulse, it has applied a limited methodology to all "levels" of knowledge and being. Of course it was Newton who gave the strongest impetus to the methodology of accepting as universally valid that which is found to fit a given set of conditions. Now it must be understood that we are referring to *attitudes*, which are the crystallized products of generations of thinking. We are not referring to a *consciously* directed approach to knowledge. The canons of the Age of Reason have been discarded by most critical minds. But the *habits* of the past still remain to block fruitful investigation and exploration of the interior realm of the spirit. For we cannot approach the Spirit with a mind filled with doubt and nonacceptance. One might almost say that the unconscious background of the western mind has been filled with the habit of doubt and nonacceptance. It is this condition rather than the worn-out methodology of the past which must be corrected. There are times, in the midst of the appalling confusion that exists today in the minds of men the world over, when so many half-truths have been scattered and where so much sophisticated skepticism exists, that it seems an insuperable task to convey the truth of the simplicity of the Gospel. Then we realize that simplicity cannot be verbalized and we remember that the relation of man to God is one of spirit to Spirit and that the utter simplicity of God and His Word must dawn upon the mind and heart of the individual.

The plain fact is that we come to God only when we have been aroused to our need of Him. No amount of argument or "proof" will convince the heart of one who prefers words about God to the reality of God Himself. Time and again we meet individuals who demand "proofs" of the truth of God's Word. The honest experience of anyone who has worked with individual souls is that there is no depth of soil for the Word to take root until the heart of the individual is prepared by life to receive the Word. In those who are ready, the Word springs up into consciousness, and a clear realization of the content of faith is born which is so unshakable that no earthly storm can cause that heart to fail. It is all the work of God. Yet it is the individual who responds and for this he *alone* is responsible. Truly in the hour of need man is *alone* with God, and in this aloneness man finds the truth of God; and no one in the heights above or the depths below can wrest the truth from the soul who has received it. It is God's unspeakable gift to all those who truly believe. Life alone can be the witness to truth. *By their works ye shall know them.*

II

Christianity Is Prayer and Fasting

CHRISTIANITY is *the* way of life. This affirmation takes on a very definite and positive meaning when it is examined in the light of the specific statement made by Jesus: "Strait is the gate, and narrow is the way, which leadeth unto life" (Matt. 7:14). In view of the over-all teaching of Jesus we cannot conceive of this way in any rigid or legalistic sense or with the connotation of deprivation. There is no lack in the teaching of Jesus: "I am come that they might have life, and that they might have it more abundantly" (John 10:11). *Narrow* must mean purity and simplicity. There is enough space for the Truth and that is all.

To attain to the fullness of perfection as commanded by Jesus, we must become empty of all unlikeness to God. For the precept is that we be perfect as God is perfect. That we may not achieve perfection in the sense of complete restoration of the lost likeness is entirely due to our negligence. For God gives what He commands, and when we have the

39

humility to accept the gift of perfection, which is love, the law is fulfilled.

No one can say when the perfect hour shall arrive. We know that we are one in Him who loves us, and He knows the hour when we are ready to receive the indwelling of His Presence.

Christian perfection consists largely in the renewal of the mind which, through purification, can once more reflect the brightness of the original state.

While we remain rather close to the language of the Gospels and the Epistles, we are not in a very good position to see and appreciate the respective points of view represented by Roman Catholicism and other branches of Traditional and Reformed Christianity as to the goal of the Christian life. We must examine basic doctrinal positions; else, when we examine the writings of some canonized saints, our understanding will be limited to an appreciation of the poetry and the ornate phraseology employed to suggest the inexpressible. Historical factors of a cultural and sociological nature must, perforce, receive some attention if we are to make intelligible that which presents the casual observer with a confused and hazy picture.

Perfection means wholeness, completeness, fullness, plenitude. All the work that Jesus did clearly showed the impress of this state. The prologue of St. John's Gospel suggests to us the way we may acquire the perfection extolled by Jesus: "And of His fulness, have all we received, and grace for grace" (John 1:16).

This fullness was *received* by the disciples. It suggests that we who would be His disciples likewise must *receive* the fullness of Christ. And the immediately following statement, *grace for grace*, suggests the gradual building up of our lives in Christ until they reach "the measure of the stature of the fulness of Christ" (Eph. 4:13).

Man, then, has the *capacity* for God, in potentiality, through the Image of God in the center of his being. How to arouse, how to awaken, how to grow in this capacity is the perennial problem of mankind. It was answered once for all by Jesus. He told us to *accept*, the basic meaning of the terms *receive, believe* and *faith*. But unto "as many as received Him, to them gave He power to become the sons of God" (John 1:12).

When Jesus said to repent, for "the kingdom of God is at hand: repent ye, and believe the gospel" (Mark 1:15), he was voicing the basic condition necessary to finding the kingdom. It was simply an urgent plea to turn from the broad way that leads to destruction and follow the narrow way. The μετάνοια means a turning of the mind, which simply means to think in a different direction from the way of the world, of the "natural" man. This turning means a more radical change than the weighing of alternatives by the reason, followed by a rational choice. This may be a concomitant action. But it is not the basic change. A person must be awakened to his need. He must call out in his heart, What must I do to be saved? We must *hunger* and *thirst* after righteousness if we are to be filled.

The steps are very basic and very simple. Yet more mystery has been made of them than, possibly, anything else man has been confronted with. And here we come face to face with the subtle and often hidden tendency on the part of man to obscure what he does not wish to face and accept. For men "loved darkness rather than light" (John 3:19).

There is a false clarity and simplicity constructed by superimposing an arbitrary concept over the truth. One such simplification is the popular and current use of the terms *relative* and *relativity* based on the idea that all is flux, that permanency is illusory, and that religion is a blindfold obscuring the cold facts of reality.

There is on the other hand a false obscurity which tries to tell us that reality is paradoxical. Of course reality is paradoxical to the physical senses. There is nothing startling about that. But the true paradoxes cannot be conceptualized, and that is precisely why they are paradoxes. Can you explain logically how the finite and infinite, how God and man, became one in the hypostatic union of the Incarnation?

And one of the great paradoxes of the way of life—that a man should become nothing that he might gain all, or more simply, *he that loses his life shall find it*—is this a paradox too deep for words?

He that humbleth himself shall be exalted. Is this not foolishness to the worldly person?

Liberal Protestantism, in its inability or confusion, has not faced the paradoxes of life squarely and has sought for an easy way out, by appealing to the popular taste for mass relief of ills, by means of social programs and by a psychology based on materialist values and dogmas.

In the last analysis no age is any closer to the truth than another. Each man and each woman in any age is responsible for his response to God. He addresses us with His Word, in His Creation, in the Incarnation, in the Bible; and He is always addressing our hearts through the Holy Spirit until we meekly receive the engrafted Word, turn around, and fully accept and respond. (Then, and then only shall we become the sons of God.)

It is necessary to look directly into the patterns of thought as they were gradually woven into the form which we designate as the structure of medieval spirituality, if we are to grasp the intent of those who thought deeply upon the *meaning* of Jesus Christ during the Middle Ages, a period which has been much misunderstood.

We unconsciously judge this period with the standards formed by later generations. And whether or not we have cleared ourselves of the mental fog which has passed for intelligence these last few centuries, the fact remains that the books *about* the Middle Ages are very much conditioned by the prejudices of the eighteenth and nineteenth centuries. There are no writings on the medieval period which are entirely free from the attitudes of the intellectualism prevalent in the last two centuries. If we go back earlier to the writings of Bossuet, for example, we are given the picture of the past seen through the eyes of a mind trained in the terms of Scholasticism. Yet we can study the past more intelligently if we know about the prejudices of scholars—accepting the facts without the particular interpretations and conclusions which these men put upon them.

In commenting on this problem as it applies to the period of medieval history, Coulton writes:

> Every system has its defects, and most critics would agree with Rashdall that Scholasticism was at once too dogmatic and too disputatious.... Yet Professor A. N. Whitehead... would seem to write very loosely in applying so frequently and emphatically to Medieval Thought, as a whole, the terms *reason* and *rational*, where the true word would be *rationalism, rationalistic*.[1]

Coulton's criticism is equally subject to criticism. For he does not properly distinguish between the various types of thought prevalent in the Middle Ages, only one of which was

[1] G. G. Coulton, *Studies in Medieval Thought* (London, Thomas Nelson, 1940), pp. 209-210.

rationalistic. The phrase *as a whole* when applied to the Middle Ages is much too broad to be encompassed by the abstraction *rationalism*. Such dangerous oversimplifications are very injurious to a proper understanding of the content of medieval thought. For example, Augustine makes a clear distinction between the function of *ratio* whereby we comprehend the physical aspect of existence and the *intelligens* whereby we apprehend the inner nature of things. Persons who are conditioned by one of the several types of rationalism fail to see this all-important distinction, so basic to a comprehension of Augustine's view of the spiritual life of man. There are innumerable instances of this kind which require careful attention in order to avoid disastrous confusion. But most important of all, it must be remembered that the fundamental position to be taken in relation to any period of Christian history is that of *man's existence as an individual who stands in need of redemption*. There is no abstract historical man. There are only souls who live close to God or far from Him.

As early at the beginning of the third century, Christians were going out into the wilderness to lead a life of prayer and self-mortification. Saint Anthony was impressed by the words of the Gospel, addressed to the rich young man, that he sell all and follow Christ. He applied those words to himself, quite literally at the age of twenty and began a life of ascetic retirement, thereby setting an example which in various forms, became increasingly popular with the gradual decline of the Empire. Many retired to the desert; and, in addition to their setting a further example, they left a corpus of writings which are called, together, the works of the Desert Fathers. Among these influential writings in the development of medieval ascetic and monastic discipline were the dialogues of John Cassian. These were one of the sources for Bernard of Clairvaux's Benedictine reform.

44

Christianity Is Prayer and Fasting

In addition to the cenobitic communities composed of those who desired to live in complete retirement, there were small groups who began to live in semiretirement in the suburbs of the great cities in the Empire. Augustine became part of such a community immediately after his conversion, living in a suburb of Milan during one summer; upon returning to North Africa he lived a retired life with some likeminded people in the house selected for this monastic purpose.

The importance of this development within the church cannot be overemphasized. For it established the pattern of precedence for those who wished to penetrate more deeply into the life of the spirit, those who had a more deep-seated religious conviction. Everyone knows what invaluable service was rendered humanity later on by those communities which, under the inspiration of Saint Benedict of Nursia, preserved the continuity of Christian thought in the West from the beginning of the seventh century. But long before the innovation attributed to Benedict, the pattern of the recluse was well established within the church. The Eastern church followed the arrangement developed by Pachomius, a less closely knit order than that founded in the West by Benedict of Nursia.

The defect of this entire movement of spiritually minded persons away from participation in civilization (thus forfeiting the chance to act as a spiritual leaven in society) was that it fell away from the true spirit of the Gospel and followed instead the trend already started among philosophical groups, of *withdrawal* from the world to pursue a life of meditation. To this end, the common practice, still alive among us, of selecting passages of Scripture which justify this procedure when given a very material interpretation, was liberally employed, the case of Origen's self-mutilation being

45

only a dramatic instance of a very general practice. The widely accepted ideals of poverty, chastity, and obedience (meaning that a person should have no money, no partner in marriage, and should obey the dictates of the clergy) are the debased materialization of the Gospel precepts of humility before God, purity in heart and mind, and total response to and acceptance of God in Christ Jesus.

This is not to criticize the monastic venture of the Middle Ages. By that time the new structure of society had been firmly established, especially after the reforms of Charlemagne and the new hierarchical relationships of church and state.

The failure to understand the full implications of the Gospel was clearly evident in the period of late antiquity. The more articulate of that era were too busy condemning the world, the flesh and the devil while the organization of the church was becoming more deeply enmeshed in the struggle for power and prestige. Prayer sank to the level of verbal repetitions and the incorporation of pagan ceremonies eventuated in that almost fascinatingly complex institution of Catholicism, the Mass. The Byzantine church carried the formal theology of antiquity to its conclusion in John of Damascus. The liturgical splendor of the Byzantine church has never been equalled in the West. Then came the material isolation of Byzantium from the West except for the short-lived brilliance of Ravenna. These flashes of late autumnal brilliance disturbed the darkening slumber of the West as it settled into sleep. The religious imagination of the West had been captivated by the zeal of the early eremites for solitariness. The desert had won. The springs of civilization had dried up. The spirit of the late Academy entered the church in the elaborate theurgy of Proclus, translated by the Pseudo-Dionysius into the idiom of the church. The leadership of the western church concerned itself with the acquirement of political supremacy; and, except for the unusual combination of spirituality and executive ability in Gregory the Great, the attainment of the Kingdom of Heaven was relegated to a post-mortem state for the great majority. The few who felt the call to inwardness had to do the best they could in a world delivered to the Prince of Darkness. Not until the Cluniac reforms did the spiritual minority begin to make some impression on the ecclesiastical body politic.

One finds in the letters of Polycarp an esteem of virginity for both sexes that became increasingly important as a mark of dedication. But when this practice led to some abuses, as happened in North Africa during the time of Cyprian, other practices and habits were added to distinguish virgins from nonvirgins. During the fourth century women were required to wear black habits and short hair. And a custom of requiring these ascetics to remain in their own homes except when they went to visit the sick gradually led to the establishment of monasteries and convents outside the cities and in the deserts of the Thebaid, Palestine, and other places.

Athanasius' life of Saint Anthony was very popular among the ascetically minded. Already the ascetical teaching of Origen had had a vast influence among the religious of the Eastern churches. And in addition to the rule of Pachomius and Basil, there was the mixed type of community that followed Hilarion in Palestine.

The increasing popularity of this exodus into the deserts was not altogether unopposed within the Church. But, unfortunately, the most outspoken opponents were addicted to a loose manner of living. Essentially, the motive of the flight from civilization was the fear of depredation and the anxiety for the salvation of the soul in the midst of a corrupt and jaded society.

The religious literary remains for this period stress the vileness of the body with its passions and insist upon the starvation of all the bodily appetites and all the interests which are related to life on earth.

Perhaps one of the most vigorous and violently aggressive proponents of the monastic life was the scholar Jerome, who influenced female members of the Roman nobility to take the veil. But his contemporary, Augustine, in a less dramatic but no less effective way, set the example for the entire Middle Ages. Augustine's opinion of life on earth became increasingly pessimistic with the passing of the years. The sacking of Rome in 410 gave him greater incentive to depict the contrast between the earthly city and the "heavenly" city. By this time, his theory of human depravity was fully developed, and he was able to declare that sin would always abound in the city of man and that unbaptized infants were doomed to hell.

Augustine's conflict with his own sexual instincts had been, on his own admission, the greatest source of anguish to him in the time immediately preceding his conversion. So it seemed to him after many years as an ecclesiastic living a semimonastic existence; but more than likely it was a symptom of the intellectual, moral, and emotional confusion of the young Augustine, haunted by dissatisfaction and anxiety.

Following his conversion, Augustine put aside marriage and family obligations, renounced his position as a teacher, and began to live a progressively retired existence until he reached the point of causing his own sister to remove herself from the monastic community which he had formed at Hippo while bishop of that city, lest any suspicion should be occasioned by her presence. It is not sufficiently realized and taken into account that Augustine became more the monk, both in outlook and in expression of life, as he grew older.

The severity of his attitude toward life and his judgment upon existence reflects more and more this monkish development.

Political calamity and its attendant pessimism came to the fore more rapidly in the West than in the East. The optimistic judgment of human nature, which had caused Pelagius' views to meet with more acceptance in the East, found expression in a type of asceticism which relied on the powers of the human will to gain control over the animal nature of man. Self-mortification was often carried to the fantastic extremes still practiced in some parts of the Orient, especially India. By that curious phenomenon by which an optimistic theory becomes pessimistic in practice, the disciplines used in the Eastern Church by such devout men as Macarius were so severe that psychic derangement was not uncommon. In fact, one of the main reasons for joint efforts in ascetic groups was the avoidance of such derangements by some kind of supervision and imposed rule.

In the West, on the other hand, the doctrine of the Fall was generally accepted after the Pelagian controversy, and Augustine's formulas received the widest currency. In practice, however, one finds a more positive discipline which, although accepting man's fallen condition as a fact, went on to explore and seek the joy promised in Christ. The center of gravity was God's love and grace to which man *may* respond. Augustine was called the Doctor of Grace because of his experiential knowledge of grace, not because of any logical theory he may have elaborated.

As we have already observed, monasticism had gripped the imagination of those within the Empire who were seeking a firm basis of support for their religious endeavors. Virginity, fasting, and various exercises in self-mortification were indulged in from early times. Therefore we may conclude that monachism as it appears at the beginning of the Middle Ages was a product of the ideas, attitudes, and practices that gradually became associated with the religious quest during the period of late antiquity.

Scholasticism failed as an attempted synthesis. And it would not receive even the small attention it does today were it not for the widespread insecurity and unrest among the intellectuals who are beginning to tire of novelty and are seeking some kind of order in their bewildered thoughts, confused as they often are by the mechanicalism of Freud and Marx.

Augustine, on the other hand, did achieve in some measure an interior synthesis of Christian principles with classical culture. This was due to the fact that he had first been a pagan, one who had came to Christianity only when the philosophies and cults of antiquity failed to satisfy the problems he was wrestling with in his soul. The *Confessions* stands as a landmark and a symbol of the transformation of a sophisticated intellectual into a soul captivated by the love of Jesus Christ.

Between the writing of the dialogues of Cassian and the dogmatic treatises of medieval Scholastics, no organized doctrine of spirituality had been composed. The later dogmatic treatises were abstracted from the practical writings which preceded them. Hence, the compendious writings of Augustine which touched upon every phase of religion and theology were considered equally authoritative in the sanctifying work of the Holy Spirit as in other aspects of doctrine. Even the enormous influence of the Pseudo-Dionysius is subsidiary to the compelling authority of Augustine over the medieval mind. Individual mystics may have employed Dionysian imagery in perhaps too lavish a manner. But the *sensus communis* of Christendom found in the teaching of Augustine a more sure and steady guide. Furthermore, the

Dionysian writings were not available to the West until John the Scot translated them from the Greek original (almost a lost language in the West at that time) into the Latin used by the western church. It was only the belief that these writings were by Paul's Athenian convert that made them respectable in an atmosphere out of harmony with the type of thought they represented.

St. Bernard's philosophy partook of Augustine's thought, of Cassian's, and also that of classical authors, for example, Cicero. And from St. Bernard we can trace a continuous tradition down to the post-Reformation writers such as Saint John of the Cross and Blaise Pascal.[2] From all this, one can readily see that the Christian teaching on the life of the spirit has been excessively conditioned by antique concepts of asceticism and their world-escaping tendencies. It is quite meaningless to point to Bernard as a man of the cloister who also participated in an active life of reform. For, in addition to the fact that he was an exception rather than a type, the end for which he struggled was bound up with the defense of monastic life. The same is even more true of John of the Cross and Theresa of Ávila.

If the findings of any of these men are to have value for Christian life today we must separate the essential, the usable part, from the appearance—that is, the accumulated incrustations of tradition—insofar as such a separation is possible. Where this is not possible we shall have to discard them and allow the Spirit of God, working through the universal Church, to inspire us with a deeper understanding of the truth embedded in Scripture as it comes to us through prayer. For prayer is the sole recourse man has to God when he desires to understand the way which Jesus said, "I am."

---

[2] See the discussion of this tradition by Gilson in *The Spirit of Mediaeval Philosophy.*

What we can gain from a knowledge of the past is some information which, understood in the proper context, can give us a perspective as to the heights and depths of Christian experience, that is of the *fullness* of experience possible to man on earth. Buddhist experience is a partial exploration of these possibilities, but it entertains only a portion of the subliminal region, that part of the psyche which does not readily expose itself to view. The knowledge of the Spirit of God comes only to those who open themselves to the Divine Wisdom which came through Jesus Christ.

Buddhist self-analysis may eventually lead to a degree of mental objectivity and peace as a result of ordered thinking. But the cornerstone, God, has been omitted. And the love which came with Jesus, the love that heals and unites, is missing from the teachings attributed to Buddha. Strictly speaking, Buddhism is not a religion (I refer to the classical Buddhism rather than the Mahayana) but a technique of psychological analysis far more subtle and profound than anything yet evolved by the accepted systems of the West. The whole teaching hinges on the principle expounded in the Dhammapada, namely that *man becomes what he thinks.* Buddha in this sense was an empiricist; but, contrary to some views, not so completely as was Jesus, who, having taken into account all sense experience in his teaching and having taught a principle which Buddha had also expounded— "As he thinketh in his heart, so is he" (Prov. 23:7)—further taught the principle of *being* as well as becoming as is recorded in the Gospel of Saint Mark. *Before Abraham was, I am;* and that all men might know he added, as recorded by Saint John: "At that day ye shall know that I *am* in my Father, ye in me, and I in you" (John 14:20). This knowledge was promised to all those who accept the Word of God.

And in complete contradiction to the eschatologists, Jesus

taught that the Kingdom of God *is within* man, that it does not come with observation, but that it comes within the consciousness of man.

The early church was not altogether without psychology. The principle laid down by the Greeks, *"know thyself,"* was carried beyond the mere analysis of the rational faculty which applies itself to that which comes from without. Plotinus further elaborated Plato's analysis of the psyche, keeping within the general framework; but, in addition to the rational and intellectual faculty (the latter corresponds more with the modern concept of intuition), Plotinus introduced the concept of the One as the source and origin of all things to which all things return. In harmony with this doctrine he taught that the soul of man can ascend, or return, to the One that is, the all in all. Now all of these ideas may be true as a partial description of the interior life of man. But it is only in the perspective of Christian teachings that Plotinus can be properly evaluated. This, Augustine proceeded to do in a truly progressive way. He did not try to distort or deny the truth that Plotinus had given to the world. But he assimilated it by showing its relationship to Christian doctrine. The result was the Augustinian synthesis. Not that the last word had been uttered by Augustine. But what he did say, he said well and with an inclusive but not eclectic spirit.

Augustine well realized that the teaching of Plotinus might serve as a good description of the inner ascent of man toward the Spirit. But it did not provide for him the sure way thither. It told him of delights to be experienced on the high plateaus of contemplation. But it did not show how the sinner might become a saint; how the man confused, tossed by violent emotions, unable to control himself, yet longing desperately for truth could gain the summit of that still tranquillity for which his heart yearned and which alone could make him able to know the truth and be free.

It is in this light that we can properly appreciate the real significance of *The Confessions*. In this book Augustine tells us how he gradually freed himself from anthropomorphic images of the Deity through the platonic teachings. Then he proceeds to tell of his ecstatic experience before his conversion to Christianity.

From this incident many have tried to discredit Augustine's experience by calling it Neoplatonic rather than Christian. Yet Augustine was well aware of the difference between his pre-Christian religious experience and that which came after.

Hear how he describes the difference, not by saying that this experience is different from his pre-conversion experiences but by making obvious the self-evident fact that it is a Christian who is speaking from the heart when he writes:

> The day now approaching whereon she was to depart this life (which day Thou well knewest, we knew not), it came to pass, Thyself, as I believe, by Thy secret ways so ordering it, that she and I stood alone, leaning in a certain window, which looked into the garden of the house where we now lay, at Ostia; where removed from the din of men, we were recruiting from the fatigues of a long journey, for the voyage. We were discoursing then together, alone, very sweetly; and *forgetting those things which are behind, and reaching forth unto those things which are before,* we were enquiring between ourselves in the presence of the Truth, which Thou art, of what sort the eternal life of the saints was to be, *which eye hath not seen, nor ear heard, nor hath it entered into the heart of man.* But yet we gasped with the mouth of our heart after those heavenly streams of Thy fountain, *the fountain of life,* which is *with Thee;* that being bedewed thence according to our capacity, we might in some sort meditate upon so high a mystery.

Christianity Is Prayer and Fasting

And when our discourse was brought to that point, that the very highest delight of the earthly senses, in the very purest material light, was, in respect of the sweetness of that life, not only not worthy of comparison, but not even of mention; we raising up ourselves with a more glowing affection towards the "Self-same," did by degrees pass through all things bodily, even the very heaven, whence sun and moon and stars shine upon the earth; yea, we were soaring higher yet, by inward musing, and discourse, and admiring of Thy works; and we came to our own minds, and went beyond them, that we might arrive at that region of never-failing plenty, where *Thou feedest Israel* for ever with the food of truth, and where life is the *Wisdom by whom all* these *things are made,* and what have been, and what shall be, and she is not made, but is, as she hath been, and so shall she be ever; yea rather, to "have been," and "hereafter to be," are not in her, but only "to be," seeing she is eternal. For to "have been," and to "be hereafter," are not eternal. And while we were discoursing and panting after her, we slightly touched on her with the whole effort of our heart; and we sighed, and there we leave bound *the first fruits of the Spirit;* and returned to vocal expressions of our mouth, where the word spoken has beginning and end. And what is like unto Thy Word, our Lord, who *endureth in Himself* without becoming old, and *maketh all things new?* [3]

From this it is quite apparent that Augustine was seeking "the way, which leadeth unto life" and not merely subjective experience as an end in itself. From the Platonists, he had learned *that* God is. From the church he was learning *what* God is. It is well for us to analyze the significance of this transformation, as it has a profound meaning for us today as well as an historical interest. Plotinus depicted the heights.

[3] *The Confessions of Saint Augustine,* translated by Edward Bouverie Pusey (London, Chatto and Windus, 1919), pp. 249-250.

But Jesus *showed* the way to those heights and made it possible for Augustine to reach them because He, the Son of God, had become man and had dwelt among us, living our life, sharing our burdens and at last overcoming all things, even death itself, in His glorious resurrection. It was Jesus who gave us, as it were, His glory; that in receiving the fruits of His victory, the overcoming of the world, we might ascend in spirit and be with Him where He is. And yet we must desire truth with all our hearts and must make a place for Him at His coming. For no gift can be received unless it is accepted. And the gift cannot be accepted unless one has made a place for it. So long as we have our backs turned to the Giver of every perfect gift we are not in a position to receive, no matter how great our desire. Hence the mission of John the Baptist to preach repentance, the turning from darkness and the shadow to the pure light of the Presence. This Presence came, and was Jesus, and is now Lord of Glory and abides in the hearts of those who truly believe.

It is in his concept of the memory that Augustine most clearly reveals his theory of how we find God.

Augustine is not original in his concept of memory as that aspect of the psyche through which we know Truth. For long before, Plato had taught that knowing was remembering or cognition, recognition. But whereas Plato related this idea to the doctrine that the soul beheld the divine archetypes before it became imprisoned in the flesh and hence awakened this soul-memory when it came into contact with truth here below, Augustine on the other hand related the memory to the existence in man of the divine image which he called the summit of the mind, that essential part of man which is in continuous touch with God.[4]

---

[4] See *The Confessions*, Book X.

Because of the Fall man has lost contact with the *imago dei* and, through this center, with God. He has forgotten God and his true self, a soul created in God's image in eternity. Yet man does not lose the image in the Fall, for in that case he would cease to exist as the image is man as God conceives him; and man cannot exist without being continually present in the mind of God. But the expression of this image has ceased in the Fall of man. And the process of redemption consists in the recovery of the lost *likeness* or reflection of the image of God. Because the image has been clouded over, we look into ourselves and we behold darkness and mystery. Seeing only by the light of nature, and being conscious only of that which this light reveals, we establish ourselves in this world with a material scale of values. Not knowing the true God nor our true selves, we fashion for ourselves idols which we worship and with which we identify ourselves. That is why "the whole world lies in wickedness" (I John 5:19). And that is why morality and ethics are insufficient if we are to be reconciled with God. Only a complete "turning about" can bring us into the Kingdom, into the realm of God. We must be baptized and washed clean of all unlikeness, of the masks and shadow selves in which we have taken refuge. And in the clean agony of full contrition we are stripped of this unlikeness, this unreality; and we can know, even as we are known, by the Divinity which made us and who upholds us by His love.

Therefore we find, when we consider the thought of Saint Augustine, that this man was profoundly concerned with establishing the truth of Christian experience, not so much by logical demonstration as by profound witness to the God he had found in the pure stillness of a recollected mind. For God had always been with him, else he could not have existed. But he had forgotten God and had withdrawn from His presence.

God did not forsake the man who wandered far, consuming his life with the remains of worn-out philosophies. Rather He led him by those very paths which he sought, because in his heart he was really searching for the truth, causing him to experience a glimpse of those heights for which his soul longed; until in the fullness of time He caused his heart to be converted to that fountain of living waters from whence flow the streams of everlasting life.

Having found the true Bread, he fed on Him continually. Indeed Augustine found what many a cultured Greek and Roman before him had found, namely that Plato was the school for Christ. For all those things which are found in the pattern of the mind and, by extension, in the cosmic structure are found eminently in Christ and through Him in God. Plato was the artist in ideas of universal proportion; Jesus, the Master of Life, whence all these ideas emerge. Plato may give us reasons to believe, but Christ inspired belief itself. Plato, and Plotinus after him, may describe in beautiful words what they *saw* in vision. But Christ, the living Word of beauty, sounds in our hearts in such a way that we know and see and hear *at once* what imagination can but dimly apprehend, and then only in figure. While the grain is becoming a sheaf of wheat we can observe and analyze its growth; when it blows in the wind we can admire its graceful movement. But when we have the seed we preserve it carefully, for we shall one day place it in the silent earth. Only the seed remains. The rest is consumed, for the seed contains the life, the essence of futurity.

Augustine sought in the form and proportion, the color, the shape, and the movement of the world of antiquity; its philosophy, religion, and art he sought, but he did not find that life-giving Word to save his soul from death. And when he found it he did not at first have the strength to turn. He was like a reed blown by many winds. Then came that sudden stillness and the realization that was his conversion—the fruit of a deep transformation. The conversion was "sudden"; the preparation was long.

The influence of the Platonists is again at work in the language with which Augustine chose to describe the soul's ascent to God. Having discarded the notion of an anthropomorphic deity, he pictures the soul as passing through seven stages on its journey to perfection. At the first level, the soul seeks for truth in the senses. Gradually through discipline and enlightenment it reaches a degree in which, the senses having been purified, the emotions and intellect ordered to truth, it is then possible for the soul to enter into the uncreated light in which it contemplates the attributes of God unhindered by the limitation of the senses. In the seventh sphere, the soul has established permanent contact with God and it lives as close to heaven as is possible in this life. It is a condition as near perfection as is possible to attain on earth. The soul has returned to its Father's house and it bathes in perfect peace. "Thou wilt keep him in perfect peace, whose mind is stayed on thee."

Such in brief, is the essential outline of Augustine's conception of the way which leads to eternal life. It served as the model for the whole of western Christendom throughout the Middle Ages. Various writers expanded the themes adumbrated or expounded in detail by the great founder of Roman Catholic theology. Medieval piety was formed by this man's experience and its spiritual literature molded by the terms he gave to this experience.

The great inspirer of reform, Bernard of Clairvaux, drew his basic concepts of Christian perfection from Augustine and from the Desert Fathers available to him in the writings of John Cassian. Following the principle, *know thyself,* used by Augustine, he taught a discipline designed to initiate the Novice into the humility necessary to reveal self-knowledge. Man should proceed by well-marked stages to the recognition of his base and fallen human nature, now marred by unlikeness to God, gaining humility in the process. Then by degrees of charity gained in prayer, he should ascend to the heights of joy and love promised in Christ. The lessons of humility and love are intended to restore the likeness lost by the Fall. Bernard differs from Augustine by attributing the cause of the Fall to pride and emphasizing the will or volitional aspect of man. Augustine had placed the locus of defection in the memory, the mental aspect of man's nature. Apart from this they agree in designating the *memory,* the *will,* and the *intellect* as the triune nature of the soul. Bernard's great emphasis is upon the restoration of the lost likeness. For the image of God in man is the very existence and reality of man's being. And the likeness has become an unlikeness through man's desire and liking for those things which are less than God. Augustine and Bernard both agree that man becomes what he loves and furthermore submits himself to his love. If he loves God, he submits himself to God. If he loves creatures more than God, he submits himself to—that is he literally puts himself under—the creatures. For to love God leads to freedom. To love creatures leads to bondage. He who loves God is drawn by a pure gentle Spirit to the heights of free activity. For he abides in the "perfect law of liberty." But he who loves conditioned existence, namely the "world," more than God finds himself in bondage to the world. And he may not realize his bondage till he attempts to extricate himself. Then the pull of this world may cause in him an agony equal to the suffering caused in those who try to free themselves from drugs. The world has an hypnotic effect upon its minions. And pleasure is bought at the price of sleep and death.

But the servants of the only true God find Him to be loving and kind, compassionate and full of mercy, granting pardon and freedom to those who look toward Him. O God Thou art most beautiful and kind! How perfect is Thy peace!

Bernard is usually criticized by liberal Protestants for the erotic language, taken from the Song of Solomon, which he used to describe the relation between the soul and Christ. But very little attention is paid to his profound analysis of the psyche. Etienne Gilson is perhaps the only writer available in translation who has attempted to examine the philosophic thought of Bernard. The English-speaking world has largely neglected it. Protestants, in their anxiety to preserve their differences from Rome, have forgotten the men who made possible the Reformation through their desire for a real, personal contact with God apart from form and ceremony.

In a remarkably lucid explanation of Saint Bernard's thought on the nature of true liberty, in which we see at work the influence of Augustine's genius, Gilson writes as follows:

As we have defined it, charity is a liberation of the will. We may say in this sense that by way of charity our willing gradually shakes itself free of the "contraction" imposed on it by fear, and of the "curvature" of self-will. In other words, instead of willing a thing out of fear of another, or of willing a thing out of covetousness for something else, it is now enabled, having chosen the sole object that can be willed for itself, to tend towards it with a direct and simple movement, in short with a "spontaneous" movement. Let us understand by *spontaneous* a movement explicable without the intervention of any factor outside this movement itself, a movement which, on the contrary, contains in itself its own complete justification. To desire a thing for fear of another would not be a spontaneous movement; to desire a thing in order to obtain something else would be a movement determined from without; to love, on the contrary, is to will what one loves, because one loves it; and herein spontaneity consists. If, then, spontaneity is the manifestation of the will in its pure form, we can say that love, making it spontaneous, makes it also voluntary, restores it to itself, makes it become once more a will.[5]

It would appear that Bernard, even more than Augustine, was concerned with the problem of the will. And this would be quite understandable from the fact alone of his greater preoccupation with the actual practice of spiritual discipline within the cloister. In his concept of Hell, Bernard shows his tendency to consider the will as paramount in man's nature. Gilson has given us a splendid condensation of Bernard's thought on this point in a footnote.

Hell, in fact is the "land of unlikeness" complete and fixed for ever. Retaining the image of God, that is to say free-will, which is inalienable, the damned have lost, beyond hope of recovery, the *libertas consilii* and the *libertas complaciti,* that is, the Divine likeness. In other words they are eternally fixed in their "proper willing", eternally excluded from the "common will" with God, and, since this common will is charity, they are eternally excluded from the substantial Charity which is God. Now God is beatitude; therefore eternal "proper willing" is equivalent to eternal exclusion from beatitude, and that is eternal misery: hell.[6]

In the second sentence of this note, we find that the divine image is thought of in terms of will. When the will, then, has been restored to its original spontaneity—tending toward God directly in all things—it must follow from this line of thinking

[5] Etienne Gilson, *The Mystical Theology of Saint Bernard* (New York, Sheed & Ward, 1940), p. 90. Excerpts reprinted by permission.

[6] *Ibid.,* p. 234. Gilson is commenting on St. Bernard, *In temp. Resurrect.,* Sermo. III, 3; P. L., CLXXXIII, 289-290.

that man would recover the likeness which was lost with the Fall.

Gilson clearly points out that Bernard derived his particular conception of the *function* of the likeness in the Divine economy from the Greek doctrine that only like knows like.

Faithful to the ancient Greek doctrine that only like knows like, St. Bernard affirms that the necessary condition of the soul's knowledge of God lies in the likeness that it bears to God. The eye does not see even the sun as it really is, but only as it illuminates other objects, such as air, hills, or walls; it would not even see these objects did it not in a measure participate in the nature of light in virtue of its transparency and serenity; and pure and transparent as it is, finally, it sees the light only in the measure of its purity and transparency. These are mere comparisons, but we may adopt them if we are careful to retain their properly spiritual sense. For they signify that the immediate condition of the beatific vision will be a perfect likeness of man to God; that this likeness is at present too imperfect to justify any pretension to the beatific vision; and, finally, that the more our likeness to God increases, so much the more does our knowledge of God. The stages therefore on the road by which we approach Him are those of the spiritual progress of the soul in the order of divine likeness. This progress is the work of the Holy Spirit, but takes place in our spirit, and thanks to it we draw nearer and nearer to this divine state in which the soul will see God as He is, because it will now be, not indeed what He is, but such as He is.[7]

With this background of explanation which clarifies the nature of the process of redemption in images which suggest increasing likeness to God, one is in a better position to appreciate Bernard's concept of Union.

"There, when silence has been made in heaven for a space, it may be of half an hour, she rests calmly in those dear embraces,

[7] *Ibid.*, p. 92.

herself indeed asleep, but her heart on the watch how while the time lasts she may look into the hidden secrets of truth, on whose memory she will feast as soon as she returns to herself. There she beholds things invisible and hears things unutterable, of which it is not lawful for man to speak. These are things that surpass all that knowledge which night showeth unto night. Yet day unto day uttereth speech, and it is permitted to us to speak wisdom among the wise and to express in spiritual terms those things that are spiritual." [8]

Ecstasy, the *excessus mentis,* was for Bernard the highest attainment man could reach on earth. He conceived of it as a prelude to the beatific vision. Yet it was realized only for a short time. Moderns who are so apt to view every experience in the categories of psychology cannot appreciate that which is referred to by the terms, *union, ecstasy,* and so forth. For these terms refer to the special gift of God reserved for those that love Him. Strictly speaking, the element of time does not enter into the realization of this silence. Union takes place outside of time or *within* time, time in this sense meaning simply the sequence of changes within nature.

Ecstasy is simply the recognition of *that which is* within the sequence of the temporal process. The mind is entirely absorbed in this realization for only a "space" of time. Subsequently we dwell upon the realization and its meaning to us.

One last point needs clarification in the medieval concept of *know thyself.* This point involves the difference in emphasis which distinguishes Bernard's thought from Augustine's on the all-important doctrine of the divine image. In a valuable note on William of Saint-Thierry, Gilson points out some very important distinctions. (William of Saint-Thierry, a

[8] *Ibid.,* pp. 104-105. Gilson is quoting from *De grad. humilitatis,* VII, 21; P. L. CLXXXII, 953.

great ecclesiastic, has not received his due worth of attention by western scholars.)

The first precept of the method is: Know thyself! William of Saint-Thierry, like St. Bernard, strongly insisted on this primary necessity. Both, in this respect, were inspired by St. Ambrose and St. Gregory the Great; but the fact is especially certain in William's case, for he has taken care to collect in the two commentaries on the Canticle of Canticles which he extracted, the one from Ambrose and the other from Gregory, their chief declarations touching the necessity for self-knowledge. Compared with the *bloc* formed by these texts the passing allusions of St. Augustine to the *Nosce teipsum* have but little weight. We may therefore take it for certain that on this point his inspiration came from Ambrose and Gregory.

Following the example of these two masters William at once interprets the precept to know ourselves as an injunction to man to recognize that he is made to the image of God. But here their influence is in a manner supplemented by that of St. Augustine. For St. Bernard, the man who seeks to know himself recognizes simultaneously both his misery and his greatness; his misery, inasmuch as of himself he is nothing; his greatness, inasmuch as he is made to the image of God in respect of his freedom. William of Saint-Thierry is here distinguishable from St. Bernard by the greater fidelity with which he follows St. Augustine. For the soul, to know itself is to know its greatness, which is to have been made to the image of God; but this image, for him, resides chiefly *in mente*, in the mind. Therefore the soul will know itself as a divine image by exploring the content of the mind, and by that very fact will also know the God whose image it is.

In what does this image consist? Still following St. Augustine, William finds it in a sort of created trinity recalling in structure the creative Trinity. Fundamentally the likeness of man to God is found in the bosom of the mind, in reason, but reason itself plays this part only inasmuch as it is linked up with the memory understood in the Augustinian sense, that is to say with the memory of God. In creating man God breathed into him a breath of life: *spiraculum vitae*. The word *spiraculum* suggests the "spiritual" nature of this breathing; spiritual, therefore also intellectual. The word *vitae* on the other hand indicates that this breath was at the same time an animating power. It may be said then that God created man as a living and animated being endowed with an intellectual faculty of knowing. Now at the summit, so to speak, of this being, God placed the memory, that is to say, according to St. Augustine's sense of the term, the faculty of recognizing in itself at every moment the latent presence of God, particularly His power and goodness. This memory is not to be confused with any actual recollection of God which might be supposed alone to enable us to know Him; it simply expresses the fact, to speak once more in Augustine's terms, that God is always with us even if we are not always with Him. At the summit of the mind therefore there is a secret point where resides the latent remembrance of His goodness and His power; and there also lies the most deeply graven trait of His image, that which evokes all the others and enables us to make ourselves like Him. In God, the Father generates the Son, and from the Father and the Son proceeds the Holy Spirit. In us in the same way, immediately and without any interval of time, memory generates reason and from memory and reason proceeds the will. The memory possesses and contains in itself the term to which man should tend; reason at once knows that we ought so to tend; the will tends; and these three faculties make up a kind of unity but three efficacies, just as in the Divine Trinity there is only one substance but three Persons.

It is hardly necessary to insist on the importance of this genesis of the faculties of the soul. It determines once and for all the conditions of the legitimate exercise. A reason that is no more than an offshoot of a memory of the goodness of God can have no other object but God. Born of that which contains the *quod tendendum*, it has no other *raison d'être* than to testify to the *quod tendendum;* its function is written in its essence: it is an apprehension of the fact that we must tend to God, and that all the rest is vain curiosity. Similarly for the will. As the issue of memory and reason it can be nothing other than a *tendit*, that is to say the tendency towards the term which the memory contains, and to which reason knows that we must tend. Here then we have the thing that God created; here also therefore we see what is man's "natural" state: that of a reason that knows naught but God, of a will that tends to naught but God, because the memory whence they proceed is filled with nothing but the remembrance of God. Such also was the divine image in man when it shone out in all its splendour, before it had been tarnished by sin; this is the likeness we have lost and which the apprenticeship of divine love should put us on the way to recover. To know oneself is to know oneself for a tarnished image of God, in which the soul, shorn of its first glory, no longer recognizes its Creator.[9]

Medieval thought on the way of life culminated in the writings of Theresa of Ávila and John of the Cross. Because of their concern for orthodoxy (living as they did on the eve of the Counter Reformation) one can find in their writings the epitome of medieval aspirations and goals. Bearing in mind that the medieval ideal of life placed monastic life above all others for those who wanted to live the complete Christian life, we need not consider these writings as exotic in any sense. As a perusal of their literature will readily show, the life of complete solitude and dedication to continuous prayer is still the highest ideal for millions of Roman Catholics. Every man has that in him which responds to the appeal of the soul. And insofar as any utterance is universal, it belongs to the true Church and cannot be confined to an ecclesiastical organization.

So with Saint John of the Cross. Behind the somber medieval pattern (for Spain was medieval in thought when John of Yepes wrote) was that longing for immortality to be found

[9] *Ibid.*, pp. 202-205.

here and now, the heart of heaven sought amidst the flowers that fade and carry sadness and longing in their wake.

John of the Cross was most orthodox in his expressions of piety. He had received a good theological training at Salamanca and he disciplined his thoughts to follow that pattern. Hence his teaching is traditional as opposed to that of some mystics whose works do not harmonize with tradition.[10]

Since the works of John of Yepes are traditional we are better able to relate them to the historical continuity of Christian devotion. Since they are at the same time the expression of a living contact with that for which the teaching stands, these writings present us with items of genuine experience which we must evaluate properly to understand and appreciate.

The fact that John of the Cross was made a Doctor of the Church in 1926 would in itself suggest the importance of this teaching for an understanding of traditional Roman Catholic piety.

Most of the medieval treatises on spiritual discipline were written for the direction of practicing contemplatives living a cloistered existence. Hence their comparative austerity. Like advanced textbooks in any field, they presuppose some preparation both in study and in self-discipline. They were not written for spiritual dilettantes as is the case with much of the so-called "spiritual" literature of today.

With this background, what then does John of Yepes think about the way that leads to life? The end of existence toward which our lives should tend is traditionally termed *union with God*. The whole of traditional literature about the way of life is concerned with means toward that end.

Perfectly in line with the traditional teaching, John of

[10] See Appendix for a brief summary of the Catholic position on the traditional life of prayer.

Christianity Is Prayer and Fasting

Yepes taught that, as a result of the Fall, man is limited to a physical comprehension. He does not naturally know God. And what little he knows comes to him indirectly. A direct knowledge of God can come to man solely by means of grace. Therefore such knowledge is considered to be *supernatural*. It should be clearly understood that Roman theology does not recognize an unobstructed, clear vision or knowledge of God as a possibility for man. Perfect comprehension is reserved for saints in the state of glory after the natural body is laid aside. Here below, all knowledge is, as it were, reflected knowledge. It lacks the fullness of eternity.

In perfect conformity with this dogma, John of the Cross says:

All the creatures, then, cannot serve as a proportionate means to the understanding whereby it may reach God.

Just so all that the imagination can imagine and the understanding can receive and understand in this life is not, nor can it be, a proximate means of union with God. For if we speak of natural things, since understanding can understand naught save that which is contained within, and comes under the category of, forms and imaginings of things that are received through the bodily senses, the which things, we have said, cannot serve as means, it can make no use of natural intelligence. And if we speak of the supernatural (in so far as is possible in this life of our ordinary faculties), the understanding in its bodily prison has no preparation or capacity for receiving the clear knowledge of God; for such knowledge belongs not to this state, and we must either die or remain without receiving it.[11]

In this brief abstract we have more than a statement of epistemology. We have a judgment upon life in this world.

[11] *Ascent of Mount Carmel: The Complete Works of Saint John of the Cross*, edited by E. Allison Peers (London, Burns Oates & Washbourne, 1934), Vol. I, pp. 95-96. Excerpts reprinted by permission.

Nor is this an isolated fragment. It marks the whole work of this author and others like him. The body, which Scripture terms *temple* of the Living God, is called by this man a prison. It is not a logical conclusion from the doctrine of the Fall to say that the body is a prison. The body remains the temple of God. The prison is the limited understanding and the distorted and crystallizing tendencies in the heart of man. However, the body was a prison for John of Yepes and his whole outlook was conditioned by this attitude. In effect, man cannot clearly know God in the body.

Paradoxically, God is said to be in the center of the soul.

And it is to be observed, . . . that the Word, together with the Father and the Holy Spirit, is hidden essentially in the inmost centre of the soul. Wherefore the soul that would find Him through union of love must issue forth and hide itself from all created things according to the will, and enter within itself in deepest recollection, communing there with God in loving and affectionate fellowship, esteeming all that is in the world as though it were not. Hence S. Augustine, speaking with God in the *Soliloquies*, said: "I found Thee not, O Lord, without, because I erred in seeking Thee without that wert within." He is, then, hidden within the soul, and there the good contemplative must seek Him, saying: "Whither hast thou hidden Thyself?" [12]

Although the psyche has no natural capacity for clear knowledge of God, still it must seek God in its center. John of the Cross makes then an even bolder statement.

The centre of the soul is God; and, when the soul has attained to Him according to the whole capacity of its being, and according to the force of its operation, it will have reached the last and deep centre of the soul, which will be when with all its powers it loves and understands and enjoys God; and so long as it attains

[12] "Spiritual Canticle," *op. cit.*, Vol. II, p. 33.

not as far as this, although it be in God, Who is its centre by grace and by His own communication, still, if it has the power of movement to go farther and strength to do more, and is not satisfied, then, although it is in the centre, it is not in the deepest centre, since it is capable of going farther. Love unites the soul with God, and, the more degrees of love the soul has, the more profoundly does it enter into God and the more is it centred in Him; and thus we can say that, as are the degrees of love of God, so are the centres, each one deeper than another, which the soul has in God; these are the many mansions—which, He said, were in His Father's house. . . .

If it attain to the last degree, the love of God will succeed in wounding the soul even in its deepest centre—that is, in transforming and enlightening it as regards all the being and power and virtue of the soul, such as it is capable of receiving, until it be brought into such a state that it appears to be God. In this state the soul is like the crystal that is clear and pure; the more degrees of light it receives the greater concentration of light there is in it, and this enlightenment continues to such a degree that at last it attains a point at which the light is centred in it with such abundance that it comes to appear to be wholly light, and cannot be distinguished from the light, for it is enlightened to the greatest possible extent and thus appears to be light itself.[13]

Theologically, there is nothing difficult to grasp in the idea that God is the center of the soul although the mind may be obscured and limited by sense consciousness. For theology has taught that God is present by immensity in all things. "For in Him we live, and move, and have our being." In addition, it has taught that God is present in a special manner in those who have accepted Christ as their savior. The theological problem has revolved about the idea of union with God. Certain statements, lifted out of the context of the entire teaching of some writers on the life of prayer, may

[13] "The Living Flame of Love," *op. cit.*, Vol. III, p. 25.

have seemed to suggest pantheism with the particular connotation of the individuality's being lost or dissolved in the
Divine consciousness. A more careful reading of the texts
would clearly show that pantheism was far from the minds
of the authors concerned. (I omit a discussion of questionable
instances where lack of precision may have involved an
author in pantheistic statements.)

In the above citation, John of the Cross definitely states
that the soul *appears* to be light itself. But nowhere does he
state that it *is* light. Bernard of Clairvaux also employs certain
images which suggest a very close relationship between the
soul and God. He says the soul becomes immersed in God
as a drop of wine is immersed in a glass of water. The drop
of wine is still in the water, but it cannot be distinguished
from the water; just so thoroughly is the soul immersed and
mingled in God. Another image that was employed literally
by the medievals, including the sober theologian Thomas
Aquinas, was a comparison of the relation between the soul
and God in a state of union to that of a piece of iron plunged
into fire until it glows with the light and heat of the fire and
appears to be fire itself, indistinguishable from the fire. It is
quite obvious that we are not being asked to believe that the
iron becomes the fire; the wine, the water; or, as in the
quotation, that the soul becomes literally the light, or God.
I have never quite been able to understand why theologians,
trained to think accurately, should be unable to distinguish
between an analogy and an identity, between a metaphor
and a statement of fact.

God as Being, or *esse*, may be said to be the center of the
soul. But as a result of the Fall, men are not conscious of God.
They have forgotten God. And, although He is within, God
remains unknown until the soul is awakened to the truth. In
their pride, men have set up a false center, the ego, to which

they relate all experience. The ego-centered man judges all things by appearances; for the center of his existence, that to which he relates all things and which is first in his life, is itself an appearance.

Because of the radical disorientation, the soul must go through a process of rebirth and transformation whereby the self loses the unlikeness it has acquired through sin and regains the likeness to God in which it was created.

For John of the Cross, this condition involved a great mystery and a great possibility, the mystery of regeneration and the possibility of eternal life: thoughts which could not lift the soul to heaven—thinking, feeling, volition, steeped and caught in sensuality, selfishness, and vanity. For man to regain his likeness to God, he must undergo a complete transformation, but nothing in his possession can bring it about. He must become a new man and only God can create that change in a man.

The process of restoration has been compared to the cleansing of a mirror. The mirror is a symbol of the *image of God*. When the mirror is clear, the reflection symbolizes the *likeness*. When the mirror is unclear, obscure, and clouded, there may be a faint, distorted reflection or none at all.

This process of becoming clear and clean (or pure) consists of throwing off, discarding, and letting go the impure, limited, and conditioned apprehensions, cravings, images, habits, and anything else which may obscure the image of the Real, the pure, and the true—That is, the image of God.

John of the Cross terms this phase of the process (the part which can be done by one's own efforts) the night of the senses. The initial discarding of overt tendencies results in a partial clarification of the psyche. But he compares this phase to the lopping off of the branches. The roots of sin remain. Following the initial adjustment and a varying period

73

of relative tranquillity and clarity, the individual undergoes a radical clarification. This last phase is suffered by the individual. He himself cannot control or direct its work. According to John of Yepes, the suffering is excruciating. Dereliction, loss of memory, physical illnesses, and other things—that is, the conviction of being a lost soul—all these combine to cleanse the self to the last degree of mortification. Nothing less is involved than a complete death of the self, the destruction of the false center of reference.[14]

While only the initial stages of self-mortification can be directed by the person, and the last phase is completely beyond the control of the ego (since its aim is primarily the transformation of this very center with all its hidden ramifications), still it is possible, in fact necessary, for the person to *allow* himself to be transformed. Both John of the Cross and the official teaching of Roman Catholicism have insisted that the last phase of purification, termed the *night of the soul,* is possible only for the person permitting himself to suffer the profound change. It is admitted that only a few pass through the change to be entirely transformed.

The initial stages of self-mortification are treated upon in the literature of *ascetical theology,* as these stages are now called in Roman Catholicism. A considerable portion of the first part of John of Yepes' book, *Ascent of Mount Carmel,* deals with ascetical theology. These stages are analyzed in terms of the cardinal sins, which must be largely reduced before the individual is in a position to undergo a deeper transformation.

The period of early preparation, during which the Novice is becoming acquainted with himself, requires constructive activity as well as self-analysis and self-mortification. The

[14] See "Dark Night of the Soul," *op. cit.,* Vol. I, pp. 409-422.

person who enters the Novitiate, brings with him a mind which has been educated and formed in a certain way. To a greater or lesser degree, his attitude is adjusted to the work of perfection. Progress depends upon ability to gain a more perfect attitude, that is an attitude more in conformity to the end for which he strives. Some minds are more pliable than others. In some, there is more resistance to change. Crystallized patterns of thought and conduct resist the dissolving influence of understanding.

To gain the habit of life which will dispose the individual to receive that for which he strives, namely perfection, there must be a matrix constructed able to hold the "waters of life." To this end, meditation is designed. Meditation consists of organized patterns of thinking which, when properly developed and correlated, result in the attitude or *habit* of contemplation. According to John of the Cross, contemplation, a supernatural activity, can be *prepared for* by meditation. But it cannot be controlled by the personal will.

The second reason is that the soul at this season has now both the substance and the habit of the spirit of meditation. For it must be known that the end of reasoning and meditation on the things of God is to gain some knowledge and love of God, and each time that the soul gains this through meditation, it is an act; and just as many acts, of whatever kind, end by forming a habit in the soul, just so, many of these acts of loving knowledge which the soul has been making one after another from time to time come through repetition to be so continuous in it that they become habitual.... And thus that which aforetime the soul was gaining gradually through its labour of meditation upon particular facts has now through practice, as we have been saying, become converted and changed into a habit and substance of loving knowledge, of a general kind, and not distinct or particular as before.[15]

[15] *Ascent of Mount Carmel, op. cit.,* Vol. I, pp. 118-119.

This entire paragraph, full as it is of thoughts leading out in many directions, can be condensed into the statement *man becomes what he thinks;* that is he comes to be, in expression, that to which he gives his attention. Thus may man get himself into the attitude, or attain the point of view, where he can receive and perceive the gift of God: eternal life through Jesus Christ.

The work of meditation, then, is structural. It involves the formation of patterns of thinking and feeling which dispose the mind to God. The process of meditation is not only structural but also dynamic. "Draw nigh to God, and he will draw nigh to you" (James 4:8). For one gains some knowledge and love of God only by drawing near to God. How can one gain any kind of knowledge unless one approaches and comes into contact with that which is to be known? The purpose of meditation, then, is to put one into a position to come into contact with God and thus to *receive* knowledge and love of God. The work of meditation reveals itself to be primarily a work of preparation. It involves the use of the discursive powers of reason, analysis, and synthesis. It is a work which must absorb the attention.

God in every case is the first to approach the individual. And since He is nearer than hands and feet, we need only accept Him. We need only turn around and face God. But it has not been the habit of mankind to do that. Man has put himself out of contact with God. God is continually extending the hand of fellowship to mankind. But man must reach out and take the extended Hand. It is therefore this reaching out, this stretching forth of our minds to God, which *must* occupy our attention if we are to receive the benefits prepared for us by God, if we are to receive eternal life and be in a position to enjoy it.

Hell is not a place; it is the total exclusion of God from our consciousness. It is simply the result of a complete withdrawal from God. "And this is the condemnation, that light is come into the world, and men loved darkness rather than light." We are here to meet God. We are not waiting for God. God is waiting for us. He has sent His Son into the world. Now is the time for us to meet Him, accept Him, and do those things which He commanded us. Only then have we the assurance of salvation.

The real significance of John of the Cross, and the reason that he stands out in the fold of Rome, is that he would have nothing of forms and ceremonies in order that he might have the *all* of God. His *nada* was the converse of his *todo*. If we forget this, we have lost sight of his true value for mankind and Christendom. We see the man who suffered mental and physical anguish for the faith that was in him. Let us learn from this example that the Cross was made by man. And, because he lived in the tradition of tortured crucifixes, John of Yepes and his fellow religionists have very often had their vision fixed on the blood and the pain instead of on the life and the joy of the Lord.

To conclude what is meant by the process of meditation: the mind thinks through a principle, truth, idea, or attribute of God until it comprehends every aspect in its proper sequence and relationship to the whole. The result is a rounded thought, a concept. When this phase has been achieved, the mind is in a position to apprehend the essence, or the spirit of the truth. When this process of thinking, that is of meditation, has been applied until one has acquired the *spirit of meditation,* as it is called by John of the Cross, the thinking process of the individual is engaged in harmoniously related and organized patterns of ideation. As a result, he sees through appearances, that is partial representations, and comes into contact with the truth.

Such is the meaning of the last sentence quoted from John of the Cross "And thus that which aforetime the soul was gaining gradually through its labour of meditation upon particular facts has now through practice, . . . become converted and changed into a habit and substance of loving knowledge, of a general kind, and not distinct or particular as before."

Thomist theologians make a distinction between acquired contemplation (the fruit of the meditation process) and infused contemplation. They insist that acquired contemplation may be attained by the philosopher who has no religious calling or by the purely intellectual theologian. Infused contemplation cannot be acquired. But most agree that it can be prepared for by meditation, *mental prayer*.

Following the lead of Aquinas, Thomist theologians teach that infused contemplation is a gift which cannot be earned. It is freely bestowed in accordance with God's hidden decrees. God ordains upon whom He will bestow the grace of contempation. Yet Jesus taught that he who does the Father's will shall enter the Kingdom of heaven.

Psychologically, infused or "passive" contemplation cannot be controlled by the personal will. For it is the knowledge which God imparts and is totally unlike any created knowledge. It is boundless, infinite, and unconditioned—the very opposite of creaturely modes of knowing. Although its appearance may not always be preceded by a lengthy period of discipline, it generally is so preceded. Infused contemplation, as the Thomists call the influx of Divine Wisdom and Love, comes into consciousness with the greatest simplicity.

Writing as he did before the Quietist controversy, John of Yepes had no qualms about resting the mind from mental acts of a discursive nature. Disinclination to meditate is one of the signs of oncoming contemplation, according to John of the Cross, and with this idea Catholic spiritual theology agrees.

When the spiritual person cannot meditate, let him learn to be still in God, fixing his loving attention upon Him, in the calm of his understanding, although he may think himself to be doing nothing. For thus, little by little and very quickly, Divine calm and peace will be infused into his soul, together with a wondrous and sublime knowledge of God, enfolded in Divine Love. And let him not meddle with forms, meditations and imaginings, or with any kind of reflection, lest the soul be disturbed, and brought out of its contentment and peace.[16]

It is at this stage that the need for greatest care exists. Many spiritual directors have caused confusion, misunderstanding, and unhappiness by their obtuse approach to soul needs. John of Yepes is most stringent in his condemnation of clumsy or ignorant directors.

The person who has become contemplative may enjoy for a while the knowledge and peace which comes to him. But, according to John of the Cross, the initial clarity may become obscure as the *night of the soul* approaches, preparatory to the Divine union. This obscuring of the understanding is a further purification and a preparation to receive more fully the supersensual reality.

With the onset of what might be called pure contemplation —for this work is wrought by the Spirit of God—one begins to know the meaning of the Scripture, "When He the Spirit of truth is come, He will guide you into all truth" (John 16:13). The point which must be stressed for individual observance is that one must allow the Spirit to guide one into all truth. For the person can obstruct the work of regeneration by in-

[16] *Ascent of Mount Carmel, op. cit.,* Vol. I, p. 129.

terfering with the guidance. It is as if one were to dig up a plant every few days to see if the roots were growing. Since this process requires faith on our part, we must let go of our limited sense comprehension and cease clinging to preconceived notions. Since some people even cling desperately to the form side of worship, their sufferings are unusually intense. There is often much attachment to forms and symbols, hence the suffering endured by its contemplatives before they become spiritually mature.

From what has been said it is to be inferred that, in order for the understanding to be prepared for this Divine union, it must be pure and void of all that pertains to sense, and detached and freed from all that can clearly be perceived by the understanding, profoundly hushed and put to silence, and leaning upon faith, which alone is the proximate and proportionate means whereby the soul is united with God; for such is the likeness between itself and God that there is no other difference, save that which exists between seeing God and believing in Him.[17]

Finally, then, we are to walk by faith. For there is nothing in this world which can give us the understanding of Divine things. All we can do is to prepare ourselves to receive the Truth of God. And this is the basic purpose of prayer. Jesus said we would not be heard for our much speaking. And since God knows our need before we do, our part is to open our hearts and *receive* that which we need. Contemplation, then, is simply the pouring of the love, wisdom, and understanding of God into a mind *prepared* to receive the gift. Nor does the knowledge given in contemplation contradict the truth revealed in the Word of God. Rather does it give the *understanding* of Scripture, the spirit of the Word, as such contemplation is a work of the Holy Spirit. It is the Spirit

[17] *Ibid.*, p. 98.

praying in us—"the Spirit itself maketh intercession for us" (Rom. 8:26).

When, therefore, John of the Cross says that contemplation gives obscure knowledge, the word *obscure* must be understood in relation to the world of appearances. This knowledge is obscure to the intellect but clear to the enlightened understanding. Nevertheless, Catholicism maintains that an unclouded knowledge of God is not possible in this life. All the orthodox of this organization have subscribed to this dogma.

In addition to the purified understanding and memory (the habit of the mind), there must be attained a purity of the will. The volitional nature must be purged of inordinate tendencies. And inasmuch as the force of our volitions is determined by the degree of love we have for the thing chosen, the central point of attention must be focused upon the inclination of our hearts. For we tend to choose those things to which we are drawn in the measure that we are drawn to them. Stated in the form of question: How much is one drawn by that which lies around or within? Does one have a response to the things which lie around one out of proportion to the need? Are we drawn mostly to God and do we allow all other attractions to serve our love for God? Or do we find ourselves in conflict when placed in a certain set of circumstances because we are not near enough to God to be at peace under all circumstances? Everyone seeking to find Reality must put these questions to himself in one form or another. And, whether he does or not, life is constantly doing so. That essentially is what John of the Cross means when he writes:

It is clear, then, that for the soul to come to unite itself perfectly with God through love and will, it must first be free from all desire of the will, howsoever small. That is, it must not intentionally and knowingly consent with the will to imperfections, and

81

it must have the power and liberty to be able not so to consent intentionally.[18]

Few things outside of insincerity hinder the seeker for truth more than vague, obscure, and needlessly complicated language. Hindering as it is in any pursuit, this kind of language is almost disastrous when applied to the simple, yet extremely subtle and delicate, nuances of the Way of Life. Equally misleading can be flowery, imaginative language which appeals to the emotions rather than to the heart with a burning need. In fact, it is only the heart which hungers and thirsts for the truth of eternal life that shall find the truth. There is no such entity as a lukewarm disciple of Christ. Worshippers of intellectual and emotional glamour will find the language of truth "strait and narrow," and such people will always be found at the shrine of the latest theory or the most glamorous personality. So it is only simple logic that few are those who find eternal life. All are invited. Few look beyond the appearance to find the Real. Men have relied more on words than on the Living God.

Since the language used by John of Yepes to describe what he terms *union with God* and *spiritual marriage* consists of metaphors and images derived from the facts of conditioned existence (which have at best a suggestive or symbolic value and at the worst a sensual content), I do not consider it necessary to take them up. Along with others in the medieval tradition, the Spanish mystic employs the imagery of the Song of Solomon. In my view this approach tends more to confusion and emotionalism than it does to clear insight into the nature of the soul's relationship to God. John of Yepes was very much conditioned by the medieval attitude toward prayer which, heightened by his own intensity, produced a

[18] *Ibid.*, p. 52.

point of view and a pattern of life in which sorrow and suffering held an undue proportion (by the standard of the Gospel). Hence it may justly be said that this man approached God by a winding way rather than by the direct approach urged by John the Baptist in the words, "Make his paths straight" (Matt. 3:3; Mark 1:3; Luke 3:4); and, throughout the Gospels, in the words, "the Kingdom of heaven is *at hand*," that is within reach.

There is no more direct relationship to God than that to which all are invited who accept Christ as their savior, an invitation to be the sons of God. Does the son approach his father through a hierarchy of officials, and are the words of his father mediated to him through a group of interpreters? No! He communes directly with his father, face to face. This is the promise which the Word of God has extended to all mankind. But such is the pride of mankind, subtly disguised under the notion that he must do everything for himself and be independent even from God, that he has refused to accept the "unspeakable gift" which is offered him. What is that tendency in man which insists on erecting barriers between man and God, between man and his fulfillment and highest happiness? Subtle indeed are the forms which this tendency assumes. There can be no doubt about the existence in man of that which tends away from God and His righteousness, call turning away from God what one may.

But that man might become free from all unrighteousness and ascend to his Father in spirit and in truth, Jesus Christ came into the world. How wonderful is the gift of freedom to all those who turn in simple charity and humility to the throne of grace!

The Holy Spirit has guided the Church through the ages since the Son of God walked among men and continues to guide us into an ever-increasing understanding of the Word.

"For God who commanded the light to shine out of darkness, hath shined in our hearts to *give* the light of the knowledge of the glory of God in the face of Jesus Christ" (II Cor. 4:6). And the Church is the fellowship of the faithful who accept the Word of God.

The great prayer of Jesus to His Father (quoted below), together with His blessed example and glorious victory upon the Cross, has made it possible for us to come into direct relationship with God, consciously and understandingly.

These words spake Jesus, and lifted up his eyes to heaven, and said, Father, the hour is come; glorify thy Son, that thy Son also may glorify thee:

As thou hast given him power over all flesh, that he should give eternal life to as many as thou hast given him.

And this is life eternal, that they might know thee the only true God, and Jesus Christ, whom thou hast sent.

I have glorified thee on the earth: I have finished the work which thou gavest me to do.

And now, O Father, glorify thou me with thine own self with the glory which I had with thee before the world was.

I have manifested thy name unto the men which thou gavest me out of the world: thine they were, and thou gavest them me; and they have kept thy word.

Now they have known that all things whatsoever thou hast given me are of thee.

For I have given unto them the words which thou gavest me; and they have received *them,* and have known surely that I came out from thee, and they have believed that thou didst send me.

I pray for them: I pray not for the world, but for them which thou hast given me; for they are thine.

And all mine are thine, and thine are mine; and I am glorified in them.

And now I am no more in the world, but these are in the world, and I come to thee. Holy Father, keep through thine own name those whom thou hast given me, that they may be one, as we *are*.

While I was with them in the world, I kept them in thy name: those that thou gavest me I have kept, and none of them is lost, but the son of perdition; that the scripture might be fulfilled.

And now come I to thee; and these things I speak in the world, that they might have my joy fulfilled in themselves.

I have given them thy word; and the world hath hated them, because they are not of the world, even as I am not of the world.

I pray not that thou shouldest take them out of the world, but that thou shouldest keep them from the evil.

They are not of the world, even as I am not of the world.

Sanctify them through thy truth: thy word is truth.

As thou hast sent me into the world, even so have I also sent them into the world.

And for their sakes I sanctify myself, that they also might be sanctified through the truth.

Neither pray I for these alone, but for them also which shall believe on me through their word;

That they all may be one; as thou, Father, *art* in me, and I in thee, that they also may be one in us: that the world may believe that thou hast sent me.

And the glory which thou gavest me I have given them; that they may be one, even as we are one:

I in them, and thou in me, that they may be made perfect in one; and that the world may know that thou hast sent me, and hast loved them, as thou hast loved me.

Father, I will that they also, whom thou hast given me, be with me where I am; that they may behold my glory, which thou hast given me: for thou lovedst me before the foundation of the world.

O righteous Father, the world hath not known thee: but I have known thee, and these have known that thou hast sent me.

And I have declared unto them thy name, and will declare *it*: that the love wherewith thou hast loved me may be in them, and I in them. (John 17)

III

Christianity Is Intelligence and Understanding

THE foundations of modern thought, that is the kind of thinking which we broadly term *rationalistic*, need to be more clearly understood than they have been heretofore. So much is taken for granted in the suppositions of modern thought that, without some classification of the roots, the task of penetrating through to the core of the problem of the modern individual who has acquired a very distorted perspective through the heritage of the recent centuries is made extremely difficult.

A clear comprehension of the foundation of modern thought, as they relate to the need of the Christian to understand his place in this world of pilgrimage, is most essential and will greatly aid in dispelling the confusion which surrounds so much discussion of religious problems in an age which owes allegiance to no accepted philosophy of life.

A few of the questions which need to be faced by those who are trying to find their way out of the modern dilemma are presented in a clear and straightforward way by E. A. Burtt.

Our questions must go deeper, and bring into clear focus a more fundamental and more popularly significant problem than any of these men [Cassirer, Broad, Whitehead] are glimpsing. And the only way to come to grips with this wider problem ... is to follow critically the early use and development of these scientific terms in modern times, and especially to analyse them as presented in their first precise and, so to say, determinative formulation. Just how did it come about that men began to think about the universe in terms of atoms of matter in space and time instead of the scholastic categories? Just when did teleological explanations, accounts in terms of use and the Good, become definitely abandoned in favour of the notion that true explanations, of man and his mind as well as of other things, must be in terms of their simplest parts? ... Who stated these implications in the form which gave them currency and conviction? How did they lead men to undertake such inquiries as that of modern epistemology? What effects did they have upon the intelligent modern man's ideas about his world? [1]

Much of the current thinking in many articulate circles is deeply conditioned by the views shaped during the seventeenth and eighteenth centuries. And the men of faith, who have freed themselves from the shackles of atomistic and mechanical thinking, must face the problem which their skeptical contemporaries are facing and understand the basic implications of these problems so as to be in a position to help when opportunity affords. We cannot win people through argument and force to the truth of the Christian religion. But we can try to understand the problems of those who stand

---

[1] Edwin Arthur Burtt, *The Metaphysical Foundations of Modern Physical Science* (New York, Harcourt, Brace & Company, 1925), pp. 15-16. This and subsequent quotations are reprinted by permission of The Humanities Press, Inc., New York.

outside the Faith and *extend* this understanding to them. In this way, we can truly love mankind.

Following the dissolution of the medieval fellowship through the variety of interpretations and constructions placed upon the Word of God, there arose great confusion about the nature of God and man and the relation between God and His Creation. No one as yet denied that the universe and all that is therein was conceived and ordained by God. But many doubted the exact nature of this fact, rejecting the received theories based on Aristotelian categories, and some began to construct hypotheses based upon mathematical principles of demonstration. First and foremost among these in terms of widespread influence was René Descartes, who reversed the teaching of the ages, namely: "I am, therefore I think," by putting forward his own construction, a reversal of the formula: "I think, therefore I am."

Men are inclined to regard the dramatic incident, the outstanding event, and to ignore the movement of thought which leads to the obvious. For example: it is not generally realized that the denial of Divine Providence—that is of God as the Creator, Sustainer, Transformer, and the One who perfects us in glory—begins by the denial of some basic aspect of the Divine economy, or plan of creation, such as the principle of "becoming," or "potency" as it was termed by Aristotle. This principle was deduced from the observation that existential unities unfold their inherent potentialities into a state of complete expression or development. The term or end of this process of becoming is called the *act*: the beginning of the process, the *potency* of any unit in nature.

The concept of potency could serve Christendom because it allowed for the unfolding of God's Plan, which we call Providence. All through the Gospels, the narrative of Jesus' ministry is filled with images which He used to illustrate the

Truth. The reference He made to the seed's being like the Word of God is only one instance of the idea of *becoming*, characteristic of God's Plan.

It was only logical, therefore, that the doctrine of Providence should disappear from men's thinking when they no longer found a place for it in their concept of life. The essential value of some of Aristotle's categories for Christendom was that they could be used to explain intellectually certain aspects of Christian doctrine. The system developed by Descartes was a distinctly narrowing limitation upon the already constricted channels of thinking at that time within reach of Western man. The terrible fallacy that all of life could be brought under control by mathematical abstraction, a purely intellectual process, could have taken hold only in a society becoming fascinated by mechanics, the projection of a limited aspect of the cortical process. Man had not yet learned that life eludes calculation and that God cannot be "figured out."

The fact is that the mental world of the period preceding Descartes and following the medieval syncretism was in great confusion and conflict. Many men had become skeptical about the importance of the intellect to religion.

At the same time, men were paying more attention to the physical world. They were reaching out and exploring, not only the uncharted parts of the earth but also the arts and sciences. They were applying themselves to a more minute analysis of the physical forms with the purpose of directing and controlling the energies in nature, either for artistic representation or for scientific use. In the process, mathematics was developed and applied to engineering and architectural as well as to astronomical pursuits.

The attention was directed outward. Men measured the earth. The narrowing of the focus of attention intensified the growth of the ego (the separative principle) and its principal function, the intellect. As a result, the most influential minds, now under the employ of rulers seeking material power, were directed to the making of means and devices to further the power of their sovereigns. The world had received the impetus of the powerful mind of Francis Bacon who pointed men toward the acquisition of the natural sciences and averted their attention from the decadent Scholasticism of his time, which had by then come to a barren pass.

We must thoroughly understand the outlook engendered by an absorption in the means to gain power for the acquisitive self. Consider what is implied by an attitude which looks out upon the world and pictures the workings of Nature from the point of view of the machine. When we have done so, we will understand the mind which formed the "modern" period.

Generally, people think of the Middle Ages as a time when men's minds were steeped in myth, allegory, and symbolism. Few consider that the medieval mind, that is the spirit of the age, was much more organic than that of its successors. By *organic,* we have in mind that the means were related to ultimate ends. The means may have been narrow but the ends were broad by contrast with modern ends. In short, medieval society had *meaning* because its leading minds were dominated by the idea that Christ had come into the world to save sinners. Life was directed to one principal aim, namely salvation. The important point to realize is that life had significance. The universe was not yet conceived as a vast machine which, once set in motion in space, was bound eventually to wear out through the friction of its parts.

Then came the great heresy of dividing man up into parts that had only external mechanical relations with each other. Men thought of the soul as a static entity that survived the death of the body. As a result, man had no vital relationship with his body. God was ejected from the universe He had created. He had made the clock, wound it up, and thrown it into space where it would unwind and in due time fall apart. Men no longer conceived of God as being present within His creation, guiding its unfoldment and bringing it to a glorious consummation in Eternity. Two things especially were lost sight of as men became more mechanically minded—the law of becoming, and its concomitant, the law of transformation. This double loss produced more havoc in men's thinking, possibly, than anything else. It made men think of the world in which they lived as governed by a fixed series of mechanical progressions computable in linear equations. In other words, men came to think only in terms of material and efficient causality. Now this is precisely the sphere of engineering and the physical sciences together with mathematics. In the nontechnical sense, final and formal causation deal respectively with the *end* and the *kind of end* to which any combination is ordered. An example used by Aristotle was that of a sculptor and the marble. The sculptor is the efficient cause; the marble is the material cause; the shape or pattern in the mind of the sculptor is the formal cause; and the idea or purpose to be executed is the final cause.

Descartes' man, a soul driving a machine, received such wide acceptance that it passed into the current thinking of France, England, and Germany through Descartes, John Locke, and Christian von Wolff. Of course these men varied the emphasis, in accordance with their understanding, but the essential features of resemblance are very noticeable.

Contrast this Newtonian teleology with that of the scholastic system. For the latter, God was the final cause of all things just as truly and more significantly than their original former. Ends in nature did not head up in the astronomical harmony; that harmony was itself a means to further ends, such as knowledge, enjoyment, and use on the part of living beings of a higher order, who in turn were made for a still nobler end which completed the divine circuit, to know God and enjoy Him forever. God had no purpose; he was the ultimate object of purpose. In the Newtonian world, following Galileo's earlier suggestion, all this further teleology is unceremoniously dropped. *The cosmic order of masses in motion according to law, is itself the final good. Man exists to know and applaud it; God exists to tend and preserve it* [italics mine]. All the manifold divergent zeals and hopes of men are implicitly denied scope and fulfilment; if they cannot be subjected to the aim of theoretical mechanics, their possessors are left no proper God, for them there is no entrance to the kingdom of heaven. We are to become devotees of mathematical science; God, now the chief mechanic of the universe, has become the cosmic conservative. His aim is to maintain the *status quo*. The day of novelty is all in the past; there is no further advance in time. Periodic reformation when necessary, by the addition of the indicated masses at the points of space required, but no new creative activity—to this routine of temporal housekeeping is the Deity at present confined. . . .

> "What though in solemn *silence* all
> Move round the *dark terrestrial* ball?
> What though no *real* voice nor sound
> Within their radiant orbs be found?
> In reason's ear they all rejoice,
> And utter forth a glorious voice,
> Forever singing as they shine,
> 'The hand that made us is divine'." [2]

According to Descartes, man knows, by means of a series of clear and distinct ideas within his own intellect, which are the types of all observable phenomena. These images include

[2] Burtt, *op. cit.*, pp. 293-295. The quotation from the hymn written by Joseph Addison, *The Spacious Firmament on High,* is cited in a footnote.

the idea of God. The argument runs quite simply: God must exist because the idea of God is found in my mind. It is a further extension of the axiom, "I think, therefore I am." Because *I* think of God, therefore God is. This form of ontologism bears only a superficial resemblance to the theory of knowledge advanced by Augustine. For the latter, in searching his memory, found God *above* his mind rather than as a mere image in his intellectual processes. Whatever may be the theoretical implications of innatism in Descartes, the capital point to retain in connection with the art of Christian living is that there is no vital *contact* with God in this kind of theory. A very definite contact is asserted by Augustine when he stated that he *found* God above his mind. Each human being, following the Cartesian theory, is a *closed* unit of creation. Knowledge of God and creation is indirect. Everything exists because man thinks of it. The ideas which are true must be clear and distinct or else they are untrue.

. . . Descartes' real criterion is not permanence but the possibility of mathematical handling; in his case, as with Galileo, the whole course of his thought from his adolescent studies on had inured him to the notion that we know objects only in mathematical terms, and the sole type for him of clear and distinct ideas had come to be mathematical ideas, with the addition of certain logical propositions into which he had been led by the need of a firmer metaphysical basis for his achievements, such as the proposition that we exist, that we think, etc. Hence the secondary qualities, when considered as belonging to the objects, like the primary, inevitably appear to his mind obscure and confused; they are not a clear field for mathematical operations.[3]

Consequently the law of becoming, or potency, was denied; and in its place a static "either/or" standard of judgment was

[3] Burtt, *op. cit.*, p. 110.

set up. This new view fitted with the contemporary concept of mathematics. As a result, the world was reduced to a system of nice orderly arrangements which submit themselves to expert calculation. All truth was axiomatically distinct and obvious to the intellect. The static "billiard ball" world had come into existence. The mood generated by the new view was reflected in the architecture, music, and political theory of the age. Movement, as the working out of the universal process unfolding the divine Ideas of God, could hardly fit into a scheme wherein even the Creator presided over His work from afar, having set all the clocks to work at some time in the far past.

Since the relationships between God and man and between man and the other aspects of Creation were changed by this view into external, formal relations, it was only logical that religion should be conducted in the attitude of decorum and that prayer should become a matter of formal petition to an arbitrary sovereign. Since everything was ordained for the best in this "best of all possible worlds," a note of optimism ought to prevail. The moral law was writ large in nature, and the commandments of Moses were plain to any man of common sense. Scripture was reasonable and could be demonstrated by means of logical arguments, one of which was the famous argument from design, considerably modified and shrunken to the proportions of the Age of Reason.

God, out of the infiniteness of his mercy, has dealt with man, as a compassionate and tender Father. He gave him reason, and with it a law: that could not be otherwise than what reason should dictate; unless we should think, that a reasonable creature should have an unreasonable law. But, considering the frailty of man, apt to run into corruption and misery, he promised a Deliverer, whom in his good time he sent; and then declared to all mankind, that whoever would believe him to be the Saviour promised, and take him now raised from the dead, and constituted the Lord and Judge of all men, to be their King and Ruler, should be saved. This is a plain, intelligible proposition; and the all-merciful God seems herein to have consulted the poor of this world, and the bulk of mankind. These are articles that the labouring and illiterate man may comprehend. This is a religion suited to vulgar capacities; and the state of mankind in this world, destined to labour and travail. The writers and wranglers in religion fill it with niceties, and dress it up with notions, which they make necessary and fundamental parts of it; as if there were no way into the church, but through the academy or lyceum.[4]

In addition to the new mathematico-mechanical view of the universe, John Locke especially advanced the notion of a contractual relationship between God and man and between man and man through the state. This view had the effect of emphasizing order and responsibility in the relationship between men and God; but, at the same time, a contract was based upon respect for *law* rather than upon love. It emphasized justice and looked to the formal outward observance of an agreement rather than to the spontaneous response of righteousness in a heart restored to the Living God. But the contractual notion of universal relationships is the corollary to the notion which sees the universe as a congeries of separated and loosely related parts. At its best this view is ethical and moral. At its worst it is dull and insipid.

In no case does the mechanical-contractual-legalistic view convey as one of the basic truths of life a process of transformation and change. Hence it is incapable of carrying the central message of the Bible, namely that we are called to become the sons of God, a message which calls for radical

---

[4] John Locke, "The Reasonableness of Christianity, as delivered in the Scriptures," *The Works of John Locke* (London, T. Tegg, 1812), Vol. VII, p. 157.

transformation—even more radical than that which changes a worm into a butterfly.

Again, it was a matter of simple logic that when ecclesiastics should attempt to reduce the Gospel to the shape of a very limited kind of reason they should fail to carry conviction and win the hearts of the people. For the Gospel is meant to be lived; and a set of barren propositions based on a truncated reason will not lead men to the Kingdom of God.

It was not long before David Hume removed the props from under the tottering framework of the deists. However, neither Hume, nor Kant who reacted against him, succeeded in extricating themselves from the three-dimensional world of Newton's physics. Therefore what these men had to say, although penetrating in relation to the views of their time, is inadequate both from the standpoint of a revolutionized physics and the Word of God. (We do not need to know physics to know God; but post-Newtonian physics has exploded some superstitions about God.) For we cannot judge what is true by the limited standards of the human intellect. "The natural man receiveth not the things of the Spirit of God" (I Cor. 2:14).

To know the truth we must be with God. And to this end, Jesus uttered the prayer which is the heart of the Bible—the prayer recorded in John, Chapter Seventeen. What is stated in this prayer is so clear and unequivocal that it requires only the heart of faith to apprehend it. No one is left out, save those who willfully exclude themselves through nonacceptance.

While the views of the deists and the Cartesian philosophers were soon discredited, the attitude which they formed did not disappear. It is still prevalent in a different form. (Hume, of course, had reversed the position of Descartes.) Locke called the mind a *tabula rasa,* a blank slate, until impressions were formed upon it by life experience. But in either case—whether the mind contained the images of reality innately, or whether these images were inscribed from without (and this condition holds true for Kant also)—this man was considered a self-enclosed unit, quite separate and apart from every other unit and also separate from God, the Creator of heaven and earth. How different from John Donne's thought, "No man is an Iland, intire of it selfe."

Descartes never foreswore the main philosophical approach which had led to his outspoken dualism. All the non-geometrical properties are to be shorn from *res extensa* and located in the mind. He asserts in words that the latter "has no relation to extension, nor dimensions," we cannot "conceive of the space it occupies"; yet, and these were the influential passages, it is "really joined to the whole body and we cannot say that it exists in any one of its parts to the exclusion the others"; we can affirm that it "exercises its functions" more particularly in the conarium *"from whence it radiates forth through all the remainder of the body by means of the animal spirits, nerves, and even the blood."* [Burtt's italics] With such statements to turn to in the great philosopher of the new age, is it any wonder that the common run of intelligent people who were falling into line with the scientific current, unmetaphysically minded at best, totally unable to appreciate sympathetically the notion of a non-spatial entity quite independent of the extended world, partly because such an entity was quite unrepresentable to the imagination, partly because of the obvious difficulties involved, and partly because of the powerful influence of Hobbes, *came to think of the mind as something located and wholly confined within the body?* What Descartes had meant was that through a part of the brain a quite unextended substance came into effective relation with the realm of extension. The net result of his attempts on this point for the positive scientific current of thought was that the mind existed in a ventricle of the brain. The universe of matter, conceived as thoroughly geometrical save as to the vagueness of the 'first matter,' extends infinitely throughout all space, needing nothing for its continued and independent existence; the universe of mind, including all experienced qualities that are not mathematically reducible, comes to be pictured as locked up behind the confused and deceitful media of the senses, away from this independent extended realm, in a petty and insignificant series of locations inside of human bodies. This is, of course, the position which had been generally accorded the 'soul' in ancient times, but not at all the 'mind,' except in the case of those philosophers of the sensationalist schools who made no essential distinction between the two.[5]

The intellectual world of the nineteenth century did not advance beyond the positions formulated by Kant and Hume. And not until the rise of the biological school in philosophy did man give serious consideration to the developmental theory of life. It is rather interesting that Aristotle, who advanced the developmental views in his theory of potency, was also a biologist and a keen observer of empirical phenomena.

However, the modern biologists often considered the intellectual processes an epiphenomenon in the emergence of the species. The exaggeration of the Darwinian thesis has led to as many absurdities in the area of *process* and *becoming* as the Cartesian thesis did in denying its existence. Whereas, before, the lines of demarcation were precise and clear, the biological view dissolved all boundaries into an amorphous mass of endless formation and transformation from which all purpose and design had been excluded.

It is one of the unfortunate facts of history, especially since the invention of the printing press, that the ones who write the most and talk the loudest, receive the greatest amount of attention from the general public. The seventeenth and

[5] Burtt, *op. cit.*, pp. 114-115.

eighteenth centuries witnessed a terrific barrage of watered-down notions and half-digested opinions, all foisted upon the increasingly literate public in the name of enlightenment and "reason." One of these popularizations was that of the man who exists entirely in the cranial process.

The scholastic scientist looked out upon the world of nature and it appeared to him a quite sociable and human world. It was finite in extent. It was made to serve his needs. It was clearly and fully intelligible, being immediately present to the rational powers of his mind; it was composed fundamentally of, and was intelligible through, those qualities which were most vivid and intense in his own immediate experience—colour, sound, beauty, joy, heat, cold, fragrance, and its plasticity to purpose and ideal. Now the world is an infinite and monotonous mathematical machine. Not only is his high place in a cosmic teleology lost, but all these things which were the very substance of the physical world to the scholastic—the things that made it alive and lovely and spiritual —are lumped together and crowded into the small fluctuating and temporary positions of extension which we call human nervous and circulatory systems. The metaphysically constructive features of the dualism tended to be lost quite out of sight. It was simply an incalculable change in the viewpoint of the world held by intelligent opinion in Europe.[6]

Now, however, this notion is being corrected by the biologists themselves as well as by the proponents of the other sciences, many of whom frankly acknowledge the existence of purpose, direction, and design in the cosmic process.[7] However, in the area of psychology, some investigators have become so fascinated by the subcortical layers of the mental process as to

[6] Burtt, *op. cit.*, p. 116.

[7] See Pierre Lecomte du Noüy, *Human Destiny* (New York, Longmans, Green, 1947), and Alexis Carrel, *Man, the Unknown* (New York, Harper & Brothers, 1935).

deny that man has any vital responsibility for his thoughts and to proceed on the assumption that man is a creature of environmental conditioning. In this thesis lies a most insidious force which, by its denial of human responsibility, will undermine any religious organization calling itself Christian. For the Word of God teaches man's responsibility as well as the grace of God. If man were not responsible, how could there be grace? It is obvious that the absurd notion of irresponsibility advanced by certain branches of psychology cannot harmonize with the basic Christian concept of life—man's responsibility before God for the way he uses the life given him.

On the positive side, it must be said that the men of the age of reason advanced the cause of human dignity. For they did not place their trust in an authoritarian religion, but sought rather a foundation to which all could turn, namely the moral order in nature.

The *philosophes* could not feel law as an obligation imposed from on high. They were deferential, indeed, to nature and the natural law, but they included themselves in nature, and thought that the natural law legitimized the empirical facts of their existence, their needs, wishes, impulses, and capacities for enjoyment. Law, natural or divine, was not for them a rule to which men must force themselves; it was a cosmic authorization for them to do what gave them happiness in the world. It was a charter of liberty, under which men as individuals need observe only the rights of each other, and men as a whole, free from obligations not fixed by themselves, had the right to master the world and do with it as they pleased, and to make such changes in their government and society as they might suppose would be useful to these ends.[8]

[8] R. R. Palmer, *Catholics and Unbelievers in Eighteenth Century France* (Princeton, Princeton University Press, 1939), pp. 204-205.

However subject to criticism may be their limited understanding, it at least preserved intact the responsible nature of man's choices. And it renounced blind authority as a principle of law.

For the medieval view of life emphasized the natural organism. While they talked about the supernatural, it was definitely super *nature*, that is heaven was placed at the *apex of the natural world*. Man was completely in the natural sphere and totally conditioned by it. As was asserted by John of the Cross, a most unworldly man, the human being has no access to Reality here below. What he is given by grace is mediated and veiled in obscurity no matter how close a person may feel to God. Also he has no certainty of salvation while on earth.

There are theologians who have tried to naturalize the supernatural. They attempt to use logic to convince the intellect of man. But the heart of man will never be fully awakened to God and His Reality in this way. God cannot be attired with intellectual trappings, nor can we invade the sanctuary of the Most High by intellectual devices and metaphysical subtleties. God approaches every man simply and directly through His Word which He continually utters in the heart; for He addresses us as He does with His salvation, convincing us of our responsibility. It is for man simply to turn around and meet God and accept Him without questions. But before man will turn around, his pride of intellect must be humbled and his delight in emotion must dissolve in the stillness of receptivity. His will must be stirred to decision. These are the matters with which the true Church is concerned. These are the vital matters with which churches must be concerned. And the men who band together on earth calling themselves Christians will be held accountable for their response. But man is judged by his response to God's Word rather than by any arbitrary decree of sentence passed on him after the fashion of man-made law. There can be no opinion where the Word of God is concerned. Nor is the Word a matter of relativity. God's Word is absolute and final. When men have accepted the Word through faith, God will grant and give the understanding needed to live in accordance with the Truth. In this sense, "I believe, in order to understand" has a vital content.

The facts of nature are confuted by the greater fact that Christ taught—namely that man is called to a special relationship with God which is truly of a divine rather than a physical and temporal nature. "If in this life only we have hope in Christ, we are of all men most miserable" (I Cor. 15:19). While man retains his place in the world of finite creatures he is drawn into association with Eternity, the adorable God who said to our Redeemer, "This day have I begotten Thee" (Acts 13:33). Through receiving the Word of God in the depths of his soul, man is drawn into profound communion and fellowship with the living God. The finite is in contact with the Infinite through the Word. Here is paradox, if you like, because this communion is a living association which can be neither figured out by the intellect nor enjoyed by the emotions, nor indulged in by the desires. No man or religious organization can either make or break that condition which is as the Scripture states: "But he that is joined unto the Lord is one spirit" (I Cor. 6:17).

Three centuries of reaction against ecclesiasticism and hierarchically mediated religion has not advanced the cause of Christ for the simple reason that God cannot be approached through reaction. Both action and reaction in the world are on the horizontal plane. The way to Christ is "straight up." Neither the affirmation nor the denial of man-made doctrines can point the way or cause one to enter the Kingdom of God.

The poor and pitiful notion of man concocted in the age of reason is dissolving in the welter of confusion which the acid of skepticism has provided. The intellect which criticized the age of theology has turned upon itself and its last contribution of division is the division of itself.

Catholic and Protestant thinkers alike have become alive and sensitive to the growing interest in man himself—not the abstraction of the eighteenth century or the animal of the nineteenth century. But the interest is in man in the state of fear and anxiety, man in the agony of parturition, man as he stands before God, man as he stands in need—in need of the transformation and the perfection which only God knows and can give.

The problem of man in his existence is that which concerns us most today. And, here again, our only recourse for understanding is the Word of God. For it is precisely with man as he stands before God, either acceptable or unacceptable, that the Bible deals. The Word of God speaks not to an intellectual abstraction but to a concrete living man who loves or fears, who is redeemed or unredeemed, who lives in the fullness of Christ after the Renewed Likeness given in regeneration and sanctification; or else who grovels in the dust of unlikeness, consumed by torment and averse to God.

It is man as he stands in relation to the Eternal One with which the Word of God is concerned.

Maury and Brunner give expression to a view of man, in contrast to the humanistic, which is far nearer the Biblical standpoint than that adopted by many professing Christians who have taken on the neoclassical idea of man in order to avoid intellectual confusion.

Whereas the humanist anthropologies (and here we are thinking in particular of the pseudo-Christian anthropologies) consider everything, including the Divine Revelation, from the point of view of man, Christian anthropology envisages nothing, not even human destiny, except in the light of God in Christ. Thus, the former judge and justify the Revelation according to its consistency with nature, the development which it ensures for nature, and they end by making salvation equivalent to the supreme realization of the highest possibilities of man; the latter accepts that the Revelation should really be a Revelation, that is, that it should be able to contradict and judge all that we are and know, what we call good and evil; it accepts that our nature should have to be re-created and not developed, that the god of our life should be elsewhere than in this life, radically heterogeneous from this life, truly another life. For the humanist anthropologies the reality of this world prefigures and announces the beyond to which it tends; for Christian anthropology it is the beyond—known in the merciful revelation of God—which determines the knowledge and the evaluation of the reality of this world. The former enclose human life in the limits of the present world, even if these be extended to infinity; the latter considers that the new, radically new creation promised in Christ is alone able to give its meaning to this world which is destined to pass away and to our life in this world. Thus, to know God, the good, man and his destiny *by oneself* is absolutely opposed to knowing God, the good, man and his destiny *by God*, that is, by faith.[9]

Here we have an explicit statement which places man where only he can be understood, that is as a special creation of God with a unique meaning and destiny which cannot be encompassed or exhausted by his existence here. In short, man's existence is comprehensible only in the light of

[9] Pierre Maury, "The Christian Doctrine of Man," *The Christian Understanding of Man*, T. E. Jessop and others (London, George Allen & Unwin, 1938), pp. 260-261. Excerpts reprinted by permission.

Eternity. In this particular, it matters not whether man is fallen or redeemed. He is still a significant being only as seen in the light of the Word.

In this vein further:

The Biblical conception differs radically from any philosophy or theology whose starting-point is the reality of man as known by experience. For the Bible, in regard to man as well as in regard to all its other objects, the Divine Revelation is never for a moment to be reduced to a philosophy, and the knowledge of faith is never assimilable, comparable, or continuous with natural experience.[10]

Brunner likewise concludes that man is man only in relation to God.

It is the task of a Christian anthropology to show that it is impossible to understand man save in the light of God. . . . Man is a "theological" being, that is, that his ground, his goal, his norm, and the possibility of understanding his own nature are all in God.[11]

Furthermore that which makes man, man, is the divine image within him apart from which man cannot even exist, fallen or redeemed.

The first truth the Christian concept of the *Imago Dei* implies is this: that it is impossible to understand man in the light of his own nature; man can only be understood in the light of God. The relation between the knowledge of God and that of man is different from the relation between the knowledge of God and that of a thing—a bit of the world—because the relation between God and man is different from the relation between God and a thing.[12]

10 *Ibid.*, p. 247.
11 Emil Brunner, "The Doctrine of the *Imago Dei*," *op. cit.*, p. 142.
12 *Ibid.*, p. 153.

The last idea expressed in this citation is particularly significant as the expression of the realization that the relation between God and man is unique and altogether different from the relation between God and the rest of creation. Martin Buber in his *I and Thou* has emphasized the significance of man as a conscious individual as against that which we designate a "thing," or an "it." But John Baillie, in his most remarkable book, *Our Knowledge of God*, makes it quite clear that the person-to-person analogy as applied to man's relation to God and expressed in the formula "I-thou," is quite inadequate to convey the full meaning of God's relation to man. For God is more than a *thou* as we conceive of the term. The attractiveness of Buber's thought must not blind us to its limitations.

On the vital relation between God and the man who has accepted the Word, Brunner makes these stimulating remarks.

In the New Testament, however, justification is never presented merely as a judicial acquittal but it is always also a creative act of God. Since man comes into a new position he gains a new reality. Justification is directly both re-birth and sanctification. For the new position is not only an act of God, it is also at the same time knowledge and obedience, the believing obedience of man.... The existence of man ... is responsive actuality, the actual answer of man to the actual Word of God.[13]

In these thoughts, Brunner has lifted the whole concept of justification out of the legalistic framework. By so doing, Brunner brings us closer to the Reformation intent which has become obscured by the brittle thinking of many post-Reformation theologians.

Finally it needs to be clearly stated that the empirical ego,

[13] *Ibid.*, p. 176.

the center of the unregenerate man, is superseded by a new center, man's true center which he receives again in Christ Jesus. And this self is contained in God, leaving man entirely free, yet belonging wholly to God. It is this fact more than any other which accentuates the need for a pure understanding of the Word—the understanding which clearly perceives that no philosophy conceived by man is able to reveal the meaning of man's destiny, man's hope, and man's source.

The perfect realization of this God-intended self, however, is simply the realization of God-intended humanity.... In Jesus Christ the true self comes to the individual and to humanity, and is its meaning. Can there be a stronger expression of the fact that the true self of man is not in himself but in Jesus Christ, and therefore that it is in God? Hence Christian anthropology is essentially Christology; for Christ is our righteousness, our sanctification, and our life.[14]

In the words of Jesus: "He that findeth his life shall lose it: and he that loseth his life for my sake shall find it" (Matt. 10:39).

Neither an abstract intellect, nor an unconscious animal is man. And in God, the reconstituted individual is truly man.

David Swenson in a comment on Kierkegaard's view of the individual in relation to society and the Kingdom of God writes:

... Kierkegaard's standpoint for Christian ethics is not primarily social, but aggressively and decisively individualistic. The concept of the Community when applied to the present life is an impatient anticipation of the Eternal, an illusion corresponding to the illusion of a triumphant Church, of a Christian civilization. When on the other hand, the Church is recognized as militant, and the warfare it is engaged in, a Christian warfare, a spiritual

[14] *Ibid.*, pp. 177-178.

warfare, then the stress is on the individual, and the individual's personal relationship to God becomes necessarily higher than all human fellowship. The "Community" is in a state of rest what the individual is in a state of unrest and struggle; the community belongs not to Time but to Eternity, where it is the union of all the individuals who as individuals have endured the test and conquered in the fight. God wants primitiveness, individuality;—hence the principle, "first the kingdom of God." No on who makes this his life-principle can possibly become "just like the rest." Each individual is forced to interpret the principle concretely in his own individual fashion—and life has concreteness enough for innumerable millions. It is the dignity of the human race that each individual has something by which he is essentially different from every other individual; he has a self. And it is the demoralizing effect of a misuse of culture and science and the intellectual in general, to take away the primitiveness, to rob human beings of their selves.[15]

It is the renewed self, the self transformed in Christ Jesus that enters the Kingdom of God. There, in fellowship with all souls who endure the like transformation, do we find the "communion of saints" in which all Christians believe. Not on the horizontal plane of human struggle and conquest, but on the vertical plane of God's will done in us shall the Kingdom of God be established on earth—beginning in the heart of every true believer.

[15] David F. Swenson, *Something about Kierkegaard* (Minneapolis, Augsburg Publishing House, 1941), p. 68. Reprinted by permission.

IV

Christianity Is Faith and Love

THE Protestant world made a tremendous mistake when it allied itself with the atomistic philosophies of Descartes, Hume, and Kant. In trying to figure out and calculate man's relationship to God, the West was inevitably led to skepticism and doubt. Those churchmen who attempted to reinterpret Christianity after the categories of the above-named thinkers led their respective organizations into a moral and intellectual decline. Strange as it may seem at first glance, a doctrine which tries to be intellectualistic and moralistic ends by causing a profound anti-intellectualism and immoralism. For morality is the *effect* or result of a profound acceptance of God—of God ever present, ever near. The moral law alone focuses attention on sin without providing the means of freedom from sin. Under the delusion that the Word of God could be figured out, the intellectualism of the deists (heirs of Descartes), appearing again in another form during the reign of Hegel, accentuated only the ego with its sense of separation. One of the greatest hoaxes inherited from that era of smug complacency was the notion that Jesus was just a great moral teacher.

The age which took for its motto "the proper study of mankind is man" is beginning to discover that there is no such thing as man in himself. There is only man in relation to God. For the true nature of man is the image of God. And man rediscovers himself only when he returns to God through the rebirth wrought by the Word of God.

Flushed with the sense of power gained through some degree of ability to bend the forces of nature to selfish ends, western man thought he was building for himself an earthly paradise peopled with prosperous merchants and obedient workmen, a world which God had given to man—but given under certain conditions which were conveniently ignored.

When the psychoanalysts finally took a peek at the hidden contents beneath the surface of this "best of all possible worlds" and told their discovery, polite society was shocked at first with holy horror. But a little later, the ugly fact was accepted along with the many other ugly facts which the modern world was learning how to look at, adjust to, and ignore.

There is only one basic reason for looking into the thought of the several men whose views have been employed by the various religious organizations calling themselves Christian. That reason may best be summed up in the question, Do these views mirror an exact adherence to the teachings of Jesus Christ? There is nothing arbitrary about such a position. For, if we are going to interpret the teachings of Jesus to mean whatever notions and theories we may have adopted through association with the thought of any particular age or group of people, we are no longer dealing with the Gospel but with some man-made version of it. Some may object that we do not have all the words of Jesus and that certain things may have been added and other things taken away. But the principle of those teachings of Christ, namely the love of

God for mankind and all that this principle involves, is clearly set forth in the New Testament; and the Life which carried out this principle even to the Cross and the Resurrection remains for all eternity the fulfillment of the Teaching. Those who would know whether the doctrine is true or not, need but to understand and apply it to their lives and they will have the confirmation. Those who would know Jesus Christ need but to turn fully to God in prayer and that realization will be granted them. There is nothing mysterious about the truth of all these things except the mystification which certain groups calling themselves Christian have chosen to place around the pure teaching of the Lord Jesus Christ. "And when he was alone, they that were about him with the twelve asked of him the parable. And he said unto them, Unto you it is given to know the mystery of the kingdom of God" (Mark 4:10-11).

No one will ever understand the Jesus of history simply by reading history books. One must be with Jesus in spirit in order to know and understand Him. And this possibility becomes a fact for those who choose to accept the grace freely given and then proceed to *do* the will of God.

However limited and narrow may have been the comprehension Calvin possessed on the matter of living out the teaching of Christ, it is to his credit that he did not succumb to the delusion that the hearing of the Word can be separated from the doing of the Word. In Calvin's conception, there was a vital relationship between the hearing and the doing. But his tendency to systematize and regulate everything did not allow sufficiently for the spontaneous expression of the Creative Word in the life of the individual. Having freed themselves from one tyranny, the men of Geneva unwittingly forged another. It is not a question here of justifying or condemning their actions, but a question of a just acceptance of the truth of the situation. In principle, these men intended well and they did the best they knew how to do with the understanding they possessed. But they did not sufficiently *allow* for the very thing they stressed so much, namely, the Divine Providence working out in the hearts and minds of believers to execute the decrees of God: His Plan and Design for mankind. Instead of evangelical perfection, that is the sanctification and redemption of our lives through the Holy Spirit working within us, we find an increasingly moralistic and legalistic emphasis. And instead of the Creative Word enlightening the heart and mind, there was evolved a Protestant scholasticism relying more upon man's word than God's Word.

If we are to be wise, we must avoid the temptation to "go back to Calvin" or revert to the emotional techniques of a narrow Fundamentalism. This world belongs to God and we are all individual pilgrims, passing from eternity to eternity. The Church belongs to God and the Vicar of Christ on earth is the Holy Ghost bearing witness in the hearts of all believers in the Gospel. These are simple, basic, self-evident truths. But they are not commonplaces nor are they trite phrases except in the mouths of those to whom they are mere words. There can be no substitutes for the converted soul. Erudition, the glamour of a scintillating intellect, the prestige of public esteem or popular appeal, these are mere weeds passing for the Word which convinces the heart and draws the soul into concord with God. Man is always confronted with God. And although man is faced with eternity on every hand, he sees only a temporal succession of changing patterns of circumstance until he hears and listens to the Word sounding within his heart.

Were every religious edifice destroyed and every religious organization disintegrated, it would not affect in the least the power of Christianity. And were there but one man on earth witnessing to the Word of God, there would the Church be. All these things have been stated many times before. The learned know them well. Those with less information may be somewhat startled, so unfamiliar is their sound in this age of mass production and mass distribution and mass membership in mass "churches." But that does not, in the least, alter their soundness doctrinally or affect their need to be stated in the twentieth century. In fact, these important truths take on new meaning in the light of present trends.

There is a tremendous urgency at all times for the truth of Jesus Christ. But in this second half of the twentieth century, the time for idle theorizing has passed. Men are no longer interested in proving by intellectual or mathematical demonstrations the truths of the Bible. This change has come about less because of deeper understanding than because of the deep feeling of insecurity which is gnawing at the heart of mankind. Already Christians in many parts of the world are being forced to close their places of worship. Some are giving up their bodies through persecution. It is by no means outside the realm of possibility that Christians in every country will be called upon to stand for their faith at the cost of all they hold dear in this world.

Kierkegaard tried to tell us more than a century ago that we cannot make of God an object of intellectual speculation. In vain did he try to tell us that we cannot find God by way of intellectual abstraction. Now in our time men have risen up to warn us that God will not be found by probing into the festering mass of decaying imagery and fantasy. The psychological god is as deceptive as the intellectual god. For God is neither a concept nor an instinct. God *is* and His name is *I am*. Deep within the abyss of being is that center of Reality which is the omnipresent God, the same God who manifested

Himself in Jesus Christ. It is necessary only to enter into contact with that God in prayer in order to know who He is. And this way is open to all who believe in the Son of God. Having known God it is for us to obey His guidance through the leading of His Spirit. For the image of God within us hears the Word, but the likeness which has been lost through the Fall must be recovered through the whole-making of the Spirit. Then it will be possible to speak of divine things with an understanding heart; we will be able to convince those who seek that "God was in Christ," for we shall know Him after the Spirit and not like the students of a strange tongue who mumble the phrases before them haltingly and with blindness of understanding.

God is always calling us through His Word. His Word is love. His love reaches out and draws us to Him if we will but *let* this experience happen to us. But we have placed so many conditions in the way of acceptance. How simple it could be if we would but empty our minds of preconceived notions and distorted versions of God and His Word. It seems to be the way of man to choose a complicated, devious, mysterious course in his search for Truth. Behind the circuitous and difficult way he chooses is the well-disguised motive of pride —the impulse which makes man affirm that he will conquer life by his own unaided efforts. It is not the machine age that has made men egotistical. Rather, the machine has provided more scope for the selfish pride in men.

Since the coming of the evolutionary theory through the door of biology and its mass application to the whole of existence by philosophers of the first half of the twentieth century, it has become quite the usual thing to believe that as automatically as he outgrows childhood, so will man outgrow selfishness and arrogance. But it is the sad experience of any observant person to see the impulses of the child cunningly "evolved" in the man and woman of fifty who often pass as most respectable citizens in the community.

Following the indications derived from the biological sciences, psychology has come to see in man more than a bundle of "conditioned reflexes" to sense stimuli. Psychology has observed that a major part of man's development and that which guides the direction of his psychic forces is the evaluation process. The values of his immediate and more remote environment are impressed upon the nervous system with relative emphasis depending on the degree of receptivity at the time of impression. The family and the ever-expanding social context evoke the responses of the child. The child is instructed to meet each set of circumstances with a certain set of responses so that the incipient man learns to group and pattern his motives and resulting actions according to the order or importance established by the norms of those who are most vitally related to him. Realizing that maladjustment in the individual is a result of warped evaluation, certain branches of psychology attempt to get behind the apparent causes of inharmony and find the basic pattern which makes the person move toward or away from, love or hate, and so forth, the many aspects of his psychophysical world of experience.

The aim of this type of psychology is to bring about an harmonious adjustment between the individual and society so that the person fits into the community. By untangling the knots in the lines of energy, the psychologist is supposed to set the person free to play his part in the social context. This is as far as thinking along this line has gone among the more influential groups as of 1950. At this point, a few vital questions arise to demand our attention. What is the point of view of the psychologist toward the basic aim of human life? What is the goal of society? What is the true relation between the individual and society? What part does God have in the total process?

The more cautious psychologist usually refrains from committing himself on the first and last questions on the grounds that they are speculative and philosophical and therefore outside the area of his concern. Yet he talks about adjustment and relations between persons and society. He recognizes that movement is continuous and that movement is tending in a certain direction. The better part of the movement is covered by the term "process," whether in the psyche or in its projection, the society of men adjusted to one another in a variety of ways. Perhaps he will go so far as to say it is the tendency of man to fulfill his nature just as the other animals do. This type of admission, which is not uncommon, whether it is expressed under the form of ego or sex orientation definitely limits man's possibilities to those of an entirely physical expression. This kind of psychology simply has no answer to the basic questions of life. It trusts in blind instinct and commits the individual to the social mores. The individual is "adjusted" if he behaves as the dominant group in his society behaves. From this point of view it is logical that selfishness, sensuality, and vanity should motivate the individual in the fulfillment of his nature because these qualities happen to be most evident in society. From this consideration alone it is clear that all who follow Christ must carefully study the trend and background of any type of thought before they espouse and use it to further the Cause of Christ. Otherwise they stand in danger of becoming blind leaders of the blind. For if the mores of a society are relative to the conditioning of that society, it is only a step to maintain that the Gospel is relative to a particular culture. And this step has been taken by many who otherwise call themselves Christian. It is a sad image of Christ that is presented to mankind for acceptance in the name of enlightenment.

The plain fact is that psychology leaves God out of the picture. The only factors considered are the psychic aspect of the human being and society. These and the relative values they involve, according to the generally accepted norm, constitute the entire field of inquiry. We do not condemn psychology for its limitations. But we must become aware of them lest we overvalue this area of investigation.

The Lord told his disciples to be in the world yet not of the world. Whatever else this statement may mean it certainly means that they were not to share the values of the "world." And what can the "world" be if not the society of unregenerate men? It is well for Christians to examine their charity and see if it may not include a good deal of sentimental idealism. The apostle John tells us that the whole world lies in sin. Do you think this judgment is less valid today than it was nineteen hundred years ago? And if this is true (and it is), how can we talk about becoming adjusted to the world as the aim of human growth and development? It would not be difficult to trace to their source the various currents of opinion which have resulted in the view that Jesus Christ is the authority for the universal Rotarian who glad-hands the world as the sign of his friendly charity to all. I do not find in Jesus or His disciples men who made a satisfying adjustment to society the basic theme of their message to mankind. I seem to hear again and again the words, "And be not conformed to this world; but be ye transformed by the renewing of your minds" (Rom. 12:2).

Behind the theory that the highest achievement of man and the most healthy adjustment is the free and unchecked expression of his biological urges and ego-cravings is the assumption that man is merely an animal. The society which considers the arrangement of its economy in terms of the greatest material satisfaction of the greatest number is likewise motivated by the belief that man is merely an animal. All the lip service to abstract ideals is mere words. The direction of attention and the values emphasized in the life of the individual and in society tell more than words can where the balance of interest lies and, also, what is the actual attitude and thought about man.

There is nothing at all Christian in the theories and values which stress conformity to the world as the goal of the individual.

Can Satan by Satan cast out Satan? Absurd as the question may appear, there are many who call themselves Christian who are trying thus to cast out Satan. In their desire to win the world to Christianity, they have modified the Gospel so as to palliate the world.

Rousseau's idea of man as the good-natured savage spoiled by civilization carried with it the suggestion that if we remove the checks of society upon the instincts of man he would be a happy and constructive creature. We find this attitude perpetuated in much of the contemporary psychological theory with its hang-over notions from the ages of reason and sentimentality.

God in his infinite love has not permitted man to sleep contentedly with these fanciful notions. Man is being aroused from his smug optimism by the terrible facts of world-wide cynicism and the complete distortion of truth by means of the "big lie" in the hands of some of the men who have succeeded in shaking off the cultivation of western civilization. It is not necessary to cite the obvious facts which are dinning in the ears of every intelligent person alive today.

Christianity will not save the world by conforming to the opinions of the world. The religious organizations that do attempt to compromise may gain a large following. But they will be ineffectual in regard to the major task of the Church —namely, to bring mankind to Christ.

Turning to those more earnest Christians who realize we cannot compromise with the world and who have apprehended the fact that each man is called to set aside unreality and distorted ways so that he may prepare for Him who is the Way, the Truth, and the Life, we must ask whether they have fully comprehended the fact that merely knowing the law does not free one from the transgression of the law. For there is an actual tendency in every man to turn away from God and follow the way that leads to destruction.

In the time preceding the terrible age into which the world has entered, it was much more difficult to call attention to the fact of the radical tendency to sin that exists in every man. But the delusion of the noble savage has been set aside by thinking members of the Church today. Their attention has been forced by circumstances to take notice of the widespread evil which men have brought about on a larger scale than ever before. Intelligent churchmen know better than ever before that ethical theory and instruction in systems of morality cannot cause men to seek the path of righteousness. They know that the person who has been made to see his distorted affections in the light of psychological analysis does not become, even according to the standards of the world, *ipso facto* a mature, responsible person.

No, a knowledge of the law cannot free man from transgressing the law any more than a knowledge of the principles of dynamic symmetry can make a man become a great artist. A knowledge of certain laws of the psyche and the concrete knowledge of one's own psychic movements does not cause one to become a saint.

A man may cherish a wrong attitude and suppress his

awareness of it by "forgetting." He may suffer from the unconscious effects of a wrong attitude in unsuspected aspects of his life until it is drawn to the surface again by an analyst. Then the analyst may proceed to try to help the patient to accept a greater understanding of the problem. But it by no means follows that the person with the warped attitude, or "complex," is going to accept the new evaluation. For the reasons set forth already, this example bears the limitation of the field from which it is drawn. But it helps to make clear the fact of sin and the responsibility for sin. Saint John tells us that: "This is the condemnation, that light is come into the world and men loved darkness rather than light." Again, "If I had not come . . . they had not had sin; but now have they both seen and hated me and my Father" (John 22:24).

The fact of sin is that men have turned away from the Word of God, "the light, that enlightens every man that comes into the world" (John 1:9), and have taken to themselves the opinions of men, the "traditions" of which Jesus spoke. Now light is the medium of life, energy and growth for mankind, in its physical aspect as well as in the means by which men distinguish the objects of existence round about them. In the absence of light there is no growth. Eventually death results when man loses contact with the agency of life. In the darkness (which is nothing in itself) man cannot distinguish what he is in contact with. He does not know what is around him; and what he does come into contact with by means of his other senses may, through wrong association, be identified with something entirely different. In short, he is blind and confused without light.

The *responsibility* for sin is in the fact that men have *chosen* the darkness rather than the light. In short, men have refused to accept the true Light when it came into the world.

And if a man *loves* the darkness and refuses to accept the truth of Jesus Christ, there is no power in heaven or on earth which can save him from destruction and disintegration.

And this is a fearefull *privation,* of the *grace* of *God* here, and of the *Face* of *God* hereafter; a *privation* so much worse than *nothing,* as that they upon whom it falls, would faine be *nothing,* and cannot.[1]

Whoever loves the Light shall become a new being. No more will darkness hide him from the face of the Unseen. God in his infinite glory will make plain the Truth. "Except a man be born again, he cannot see the kingdom of God" (John 3:3).

The glorious view that is held before the soul of man, that he may become partaker of the divine nature, is the real reason for man's presence here upon earth. Jesus did not come merely to save men from death. He came and brought with Him the possibility of a man's becoming the son of God by partaking of the divine nature.

There is no other way to life, to truth, to God, except by way of accepting Jesus Christ, the Word of God. Either we seek to harmonize with and conform to the world and sink into nothingness, or else we turn to God and "seek [Him] while He may be found" (Isa. 55:6). Life or death—we are faced with this absolute choice and the responsibility is with each individual. No one can make the choice for another. He who chooses God will find a new life, a new consciousness, a new understanding gradually coming to birth in his existence. He will come to *know* the meaning of the words "I live; yet not I, but Christ liveth in me" (Gal. 2:20). Then he will dis-

[1] John Donne, "A Sermon preached to the King's Majestie at Whitehall, 24 Febr. 1625," *Complete Poetry and Selected Prose,* edited by John Hayward (Bloomsbury, Nonesuch Press, 1929), pp. 557-558.

cover that the torment in his life was the call of God to turn into the way of peace. Who can fathom the stillness that fills the soul who meets his God? Who can comprehend the measureless light of love which transforms the understanding of the mind and causes the spirit to search the deep things of God? He who hears the sound of the interior Word will find his life becoming a song in the realm of God.

No one can speak of the mysteries of transformation. For they are the heritage of the sons of God. Then are they mysteries no more, but clear light, in those who have the mind of Christ.

Behind every statement Jesus uttered stands the mystery of the Kingdom of God.

We strive and struggle to comprehend this mystery. Perhaps we give up, as the rationalists have done, and try to explain it away in purely eschatological terms. But Jesus said the Kingdom of God is within the reach of every man who will accept it. Since the Kingdom is within us, the only thing that remains for us to do in order to know this truth is to become conscious of it. To ask why only a few have realized the truth of this statement in the nearly two thousand years since the Advent is parallel to asking the question, Why was Jesus not accepted as the Son of God when he lived among men and performed the miracles recorded in the Gospels? Why do men love darkness rather than light? There can be no *reason* for these things any more than there can be reason for a man to take his own life. God has called men to everlasting life in perfect communion with Himself. That is all that interests the Christian. It is quite irrelevant that he should spend his time speculating about facts which do not yield to reason. The true Christian is so filled with love for God and His Kingdom that he has no time for idle speculation of this sort.

Let the Word of God *dissolve confusion and misunderstanding*.

The fact of sin is plain; and in the light of the Gospel it is evident where the responsibility for sin lies. If one were to put it very simply, sin appears in a human life when the seeming is chosen instead of the real. By judging from appearances, the individual misses the path of righteousness. "Judge not according to the appearance, but judge righteous judgment" (John 7:24).

Since man was created in the image and likeness of God, the "first" occasion of sin was the choice of acting contrary to his own essential nature. By so doing, man not only disobeyed God but violated his own nature and natural tendency, which tendency is to choose what God ordains for the good of His creation.

By turning away from God and loving the "darkness," man has become so used to the world of shades and "ghosts" that he is blinded by the light of truth when it comes into his existence. He has lost the use of his ability to see the truth, and, like a man under a spell, he no longer remembers God or his own true self.

It is from this point of view that we can understand why Augustine used the images of forgetting and remembering in the tenth chapter of the *Confessions*, as well as his use of the concept of spiritual illumination which he based on the prologue of John's Gospel and developed into his delineation of the seven stages of the soul's return to God. In the sixth stage, the soul enters the "marvellous light" of God. The enlightenment follows the attainment of calm and peace in the "fifth" stage of the soul's journey.

It is very limited and anthropomorphic to imagine God as a taskmaster who arbitrarily imposes a duty upon man as though he were a slave who is merely told what to do and then is punished severely if he does not adhere to his assigned task.

God knows the plan of His creation so that each part works together to form a perfect whole—not as the parts of a machine but as the parts of a vine which cannot be separated, in structure and function, from their relative part in the life of the organism. God cares for the vine.

Men chose to separate from the vine of life. Hence their need of salvation. For he needs to be saved who has lost the way of life, not he who is firmly upon it. God sent his Son into the world that men might be restored to their rightful place in the Divine Plan.

We have dwelt already on the element of choice and responsibility in the context of sin. But there remains the fact of need and the realization of need. First we must set out the need in its broadest application. And, as already stated, man needs to find his way back to God's Plan. There can be no doubt about the existence of God's Plan. The whole universe testifies to it. And every man who has been born again of God testifies to it. There is no other way of proving the existence of God and His Plan. One cannot prove it by mere words. Even the inspired words of Scripture mean nothing until the heart has been awakened to the living Reality within them. The most that can be done by means of words is to conceive images which by their clarity and symbolic value are able to act as sparks to the mind *prepared* for the enlightening. Man needs to find his way back to God who is inseparable from His Plan. For by His Mind, Being, and Love, He sustains it and brings it to fulfillment in eternity.

Having stated the need, we must consider what the individual must do to retrace his steps. He must find the Plan if he is to know it and live in harmony with it. Since the Plan is neither a blueprint laid away in some dimensional condition nor is it a pillar of stone with some maxims inscribed on it, it can be found only where it *is*, namely, in the Kingdom of God within every human heart. That is where every man who seeks shall find it. And were he to read every book that has ever been written or visit every time and place that has ever existed, even were he to meet Jesus Christ in the flesh, he would be referred to the God who dwells in a place "set apart" within the center of his being. "For ye are the temples of the living God; as God hath said, I will dwell in them" (II Cor. 6:16).

Every man must make the Word of salvation his own. The Word is God's Plan. "All things were made by Him" (John 1:3). And then the individual must realize his responsibility as well as his possibility. Now faith is continually stressed as the key that unlocks the gate of heaven. But what is faith? Preachers are constantly exhorting people from the pulpits to have faith, as though it were some vague nebulous condition of passivity in which God is supposed to work wonders and make everything all right. Faith is no such thing. Faith is the spirit of divine acceptance which, when it enters a man's consciousness, makes a fact of his spiritual possibility. There are no mysteries *within* the Kingdom of God. The mysteries are all on the outside looking in. This statement is not so startling when it is associated with faith. At first we know only of the possibility of a certain condition. What it actually may be, or what it may involve, is all a matter of conjecture. In short, it is a mystery. But once we have *fully entered into* the substance of that which we only knew as existing in the realm of possibility, the mystery ceases. "For now we see through a glass, darkly; but then face to face" (I Cor. 13:12). This perspective toward mystery and the character of faith is void of all glamour and mysticism. It may seem downright plain. But faith and the Kingdom of God are absolute Realities. We do not find them nor are we aided by fancy language or obscure, involved phraseology. In this discussion, the author has tried his best to stay close to the simplest, clearest language, realizing that the best directive is a clear usable one, rather than an ornate technical one.

When Jesus spoke to his disciples and said to them, "The words that I speak unto you, they are spirit, and they are life," he could hardly have been referring to the sound vibrations that impinged on the tympanums of his listeners' ears. Jesus was Reality-minded, and every word he uttered came filled with the consciousness of life and truth. And he who received them then and who receives them now in *faith* will come to know not only the words but Him who spoke them.

In the Reformation Period, prior to the mechanical universe invented in the seventeenth century, men in religion still thought of God as omnipresent to His creation. The world and the lives of men were filled with a moving, dynamic purpose.

God revealed Himself in the Bible as the *One Who Is;* and the nature of Him who truly *is,* is love. All of God's creation is *that which is,* because He has *given* it existence and being. Lastly, God who is Love by nature, gives the Son of His Love to all who will receive Him in love, that they may be "partakers of the divine nature" (II Pet. 1:4). And this is possible because God has created *each* man in the image and likeness of Himself. He confers Being upon beings who, through the regeneration of His love, are translated into the Kingdom of His dear Son. We cannot lose the divine image. For this is our *being,* or essence, and through the regeneration of Christ we enter into a relationship with God which is simply inconceivable to the human intellect. We can bear witness to it only when we have entered into the realm of

God. All the attempts to describe the gift of God stand in danger of serious and fatal misunderstanding. It is somewhat similar to trying to explain the beauties of Bach's B minor Mass to a man born deaf.

Yet so long as we are going to use language to convey some meaning, we must have real referents. The basic Reality is the *existence* of God. God *is*. And in immediate sequence to this basic reality, I *am*. These are the basic facts with which every man has to deal. And it was this which prompted Augustine to write that he wanted only to know God and his own soul.

A man who thought in terms of the mechanistic cosmology would naturally think this a very narrow and impossible position to take. God for him is outside of the universe. The "soul" is locked up in the brain. All that can be known is presented to him in the realm of extension. But for Augustine, God was the God of the Bible. God was for him the only real *existence*. And this God had given him existence. Through Adam's fall, men have lapsed from their true condition. They no longer know God. Neither do they know their true selves, the being which God gave them in the beginning. Hence Augustine was stating what every Christian really means when he seeks salvation. For we can only *really* know God and our own souls when, through faith, we have accepted Jesus Christ, at the center of our being, and have allowed Him to change our lives from sin and unlikeness to Him into the radiant image of His Glory which shines from everlasting to everlasting. In this state, only, is true knowledge possible. For we have then been cleared of the astigmatic vision with which we looked at life before.

It has taken the corrosive influence of David Hume and Feuerbach to undermine the false assurance of mechanism, although they were themselves caught within the atomistic pattern. It has taken novelists like Dostoyevsky to reveal the unpleasant depths beneath the respectable ego of the society nurtured on gods of the "Enlightenment." There is still a vast amount of naïve confidence that the physical sciences can lead the way out of insecurity and doubt. But this is just a "hang-over" from the past, an opinion which the generality of mankind has accepted along with the many other delusions and illusions which are passed on to each generation by force of habit and the automatism of the unregenerate mentality.

The desire to make systems does not deter even the cynic. Spengler, in fact, has erected a system based on cynicism. For him, all motives are rooted in the biological impulses of the race which follow a natural cycle, fixed and determined. For him, the value of history lies in the possibility of charting the recurrent cycles of culture and civilization which exist to mark off the development of "prime symbols," that which the race is destined to unfold in its life sequence.[2]

Arnold Toynbee is much nearer a Christian point of view in his great work *A Study of History*. Toynbee recognizes a pattern of development in all the civilizations of mankind in the past. But there is no deterministic cycle in his concept of history. He sees civilization as the total pattern of relationships between individuals—individuals who are responsible for their choices and who through their decisions and resulting actions determine for themselves the way that their civilization shall go.

It is doubtful whether Toynbee's ideas will find a receptive matrix to contain and develop them. There is too strong a leaning in the direction of positivism, of the type of Auguste Comte, for a more Christian interpretation of history to be accepted by the academic mind of today. Not that Comte's

[2] See Oswald Spengler, *The Decline of the West* (New York, Knopf, 1927-28), Vol. I.

views are accepted literally in place of Toynbee's. (For Comte was a philosopher of history as well as a sociologist.) But there is a stronger tendency to conceive of society as an evolving entity with the individual reduced to the status of a function of his environment. Empirical science replaces metaphysics as the criterion of knowledge.

The Christian must take his stand on the fundamental fact of the Being of God and his own existence in that Being who upholds, sustains, and brings to fruition the plan of redemption for as many who, by their own free choice, accept the will of God. The Christian does not stand outside of society. He stands within society, not as a function of the environment, but as a living member of mankind. He is within, yet above, history. For he lives in God who is above history yet within it. The Christian stands between Time and Eternity. When he is mature, he is a citizen of heaven as well as of the earth.

But it is impossible to approach and picture with any degree of meaning that which truly exists in the Christian so long as we cling to the kind of false intellectualism which regards the individual in terms of split-up segments. We must see each other as we really are—individual souls approaching God who is our very Being; or, conversely, individuals who are withdrawing from God, the source of all being and existence.

We are not vegetables, nor are we mechanisms. God sees us whole and perfect, as we exist in Him. It is we who make ourselves *unknown* to God by falling away from perfection. God knows us in salvation. So to know God is more precisely to be known by God—*knowing in being known*.

When we have regained the likeness which we had with God in the beginning then also do we realize our true existence in Him. This fact presents a paradox to common sense.

But to be a Christian means, among other things, to acquire an "uncommon" sense.

These things which we write in paradox are extremely simple in actuality—so simple that we do not turn to them and realize their meaning until we awaken to our basic needs. What is more simple than the omnipresence of God—yet we do not turn to God until we realize our need of Him.

The inner spiritual movement of Protestant Christianity has often been attacked through lack of understanding of its dynamic. There are those who maintain that Reformation spirituality is essentially quietistic because it denies the value of works. On the other hand there are those who claim that Protestantism is activistic, absorbed in externality—in the attempt to change the world by various kinds of legislated reforms, social programs, and morality campaigns. These two extremes of criticism have adequate justification on the basis of an observation of the lives of many who call themselves Christian.

In answer to the first charge, heard most often in Roman Catholic quarters, it must be definitely asserted that the Protestant ethos is positive and affirmative, the very thing which quietism is not. But the positive quality of its spirituality lies in its emphasis upon wholehearted *response* to the Word of God, spoken in Christ, revealed in Scripture, and spoken again in the hearts of all believers through the indwelling of the Holy Spirit. Our response consists in *allowing* the Word of God to speak in and through us. In permitting this spiritual activity to take place within us until the light of Christ has filled our lives and radiates through us, unobstructedly, to the benefit of mankind, we have fulfilled our responsibility. There is nothing negative or quietistic in this. For the true response requires us to be alert at all times to the prompting of the Spirit. We are required to trust God in all things and self in none. Nor could we do this of ourselves. But we have the assurance of the Scripture that it is "God which worketh in you both to will and to do of his good pleasure" (Phil. 2:13).

There are those who think that when the Protestant says he believes in Christ, he is simply giving his approval to the position maintained by some religious body in the same attitude that he might say he believed in Einstein's theory of relativity. This criticism is rightly directed against many within the bounds of Protestant orthodoxy who do have this attitude. Their lives and their Christian experience show forth the poverty of their understanding.

The kind of acceptance and response which is of the very essence of Christianity is clear, simple, direct, unmediated by ritualistic symbols. It is the response of life to Life, of love to Love, of light to Light. It is entirely free from emotionalism of any kind. It has nothing to do with yearnings and longings for an absent Beloved. For God does not play games with the human soul. The promise of Scripture is that those who fully accept, that is have faith, shall be made partakers of the Divine Nature.

Anders Nygren rightly scores the mistaken belief that man can climb up into God of his own unaided will, a view which has sometimes been associated with Catholic piety. Nygren is not entirely sound in his position and his work *Agape and Eros* stands in need of considerable correction. However, he does rightly stress that salvation is *given* to man in the Incarnation, that man has not earned the gift of God; it is freely given. Luther's great insight (and this is Nygren's theme) was the free gift of God to all who believed on Christ.

"Well now! my God has given to me, unworthy and lost man, without any merit, absolutely for nothing and out of pure mercy, through and in Christ, the full riches of all godliness (Frömmigkeit) and blessedness, so that I henceforth need nothing more than to believe it is so. Well then, for such a Father, who has so prodigally lavished upon me His blessings, I will in return freely, joyously and for nothing do what is well-pleasing to him, and also be a Christian towards my neighbour, as Christ has been to me." [3]

The key to the understanding of this passage which is so simple, yet in need of careful treatment, is in the words "to believe it is so." Contrary to the false opinion that this is a verbal assent, we must affirm that it is the most positive act of which man is capable. And fully to believe reaches down into the depths of man's soul and brings about a complete revolution of life. The new life which follows the acceptance of Christ is an act of gratitude and thanksgiving for the gift so freely given.

N. P. Williams in his book *The Grace of God* makes a distinction between the "once-born" and the "twice-born" Christian. (He was not the first to think of such an antinomy.) The "twice-born" Christian has gone through a sudden change of a very radical nature which leaves the man different in certain fundamental respects. He uses Paul and Augustine as examples. However, it needs to be pointed out that such "sudden" changes have a long background of struggle and conflict as is evident both in the case of Paul and Augustine. Williams' conception of a "once-born" Christain makes one think of the admonition, "Because thou art lukewarm, and neither cold nor hot, I will spew thee out of my mouth" (Rev. 3:16).

Profound faith in God may appear suddenly. But in most instances there are many crises and struggles before a complete turning to God is evident. For there is an element in

---

[3] Anders Nygren, *Agape and Eros* (New York, Macmillan, 1939), Vol. II, a quotation from Luther, cited in a footnote.

man which resists God until the very end. Only at the end is the "new man" completely victorious over the "old man." And then, the glory is of God, as well as the victory. "But thanks be to God, which giveth us the victory through our lord Jesus Christ" (I Cor. 15:57).

Through the knowledge given to us by the Word of God, namely, the basic truth of our existence in God who is our very life, "For in Him we live, and move, and have our being," we are in a position to take to ourselves the free gift of God, and through the exercise of positive faith, to become established in the realization that "Now are we the sons of God."

It is at this point that the significance of the testimony of the saints we have discussed in this book becomes evident. For Augustine, Bernard, and John of the Cross, the three men whose ideas of Christianity as the way unto life have dominated both Protestant and Catholic thinking, our goal on earth is to remember God and through Him, our true selves, whom we have forgotten. The ascetic disciplines, the attainment of humility and charity (the foundation and the roof of the Christian life as Saint Francis of Sales wrote to Saint Jane Frances of Chantal), were conceived as necessary steps in the process of *recovering* the consciousness of Him whom we have forgotten. They realized, from *experience,* that they had to become empty of self in order to be filled with Christ.

Not only these men, but even the Epistles, are full of references to our *growth* in grace. They remind us that the life of regeneration is a constant process and men become saints only when they have persevered to the end. It is the lack of understanding of this particular point which is the cause of so much confusion in the types of Protestant religion which attempt to convert people by overwhelming them with emotional appeals gauged to rouse their fears of damnation.

It is a well-known fact that those who have been "converted" by these emotional appeals frequently revert to their former condition, with the additional confusion introduced by an emotional crisis which remains unassimilated.

Profound faith establishes a stillness in the heart which nothing can take away. No matter how much personal suffering the Christian may endure, and he inevitably endures much, it is always on the outside of his faith. There is a depth within his being where only God is. And he most vividly realizes this when, paradoxically, his life is most exposed to the cross of darkness and misunderstanding. We think in dramatic terms and imagine that spectacular physical torture is the form of suffering endured by Christian saints. But that is a pale shadow of the suffering of the saints. No one knows how they suffer because it is all done in silence and simplicity. There are no dramatics in the life of the saint. He is completely unknown even when he is known. And the greater the Christian, the more invisible he is. For he is most near to God who is most invisible.

The life of agape. It streams out of silence and pours itself into the hearts and minds of men without their knowing it. God is most gracious to those who are least deserving. And if they respond, they can become His saints.

God is all love. It is we who judge ourselves when we fail to respond.

If you would know God, face Jesus Christ.

Maturity is always simple, as was the earthly life of Jesus Christ. And the love, the simple love, which He released into the world is carried on in His Church. God can do no more than He has done, that is to reveal Himself and to give Himself so that all who will may receive eternal life.

Men will never succeed in their attempts to make a system

of the love of God. And God does not favor the theologian with His grace more than He does the humble peasant or fisherman who might perhaps listen to and hear and heed His Word.

Behind the theology of Augustine, of Bernard, of John of Yepes, is the simple fact that the man who would know God must turn his attention to Him. The saints know God because they completely turn to Him. Anything they may write, which later generations classify as theology, is written in the presence of God or apart from God. Men are called saints because they have so lived in God's presence that at the end all that we see in them is the light of His countenance.

Instead of being so entirely absorbed in the multiplicity of terms, categories, images, comparisons, and so forth, which men of God used to convey a reflection of that which they apprehended in spirit and in truth, we should study what it was that made it possible for them to become the saints of the Church. Especially we should note the *quality* of attention to which they attained.

We cannot hide behind the doctrine of the sovereign will of God as the explanation for the glorious achievements of these men and women in the past. They quite simply attended to God with all their capacity. It was God who made this concentration possible. But He gives the power to become His sons to as many as receive His only begotten Son.

Augustine used the terminology of the Platonists to describe his experience of Christian witness; Bernard used many of the terms employed by the Desert Fathers; John of the Cross couched his expressions with imagery drawn from all these as well as from Dionysius and the Scholastics. But their theme is the theme of every Christian—the finding of God through Jesus Christ.

The Church can never commit itself to any man-made

system of theology as the definite statement of the content of Christian Faith. Such a commitment would, in fact, constitute a basic contradiction of the tenets of the Reformation —indeed of the Gospel, of the Word of God. It is for us to understand the Word of God—and that ever more deeply, ever more completely. But understanding is an individual affair. For God always addresses Himself directly to each individual, calling him to repentance and to the fullness of life in Christ Jesus.

These basic simplicities, these basic verities, must be affirmed in every generation. Jesus Christ calls us to bear witness. Let us all become His saints. There never has been a time when the world so deeply needed the Son of God. The urgency is perhaps beyond the possibility of comprehension. Yet there is only one way to establish Christianity and that is for every believer to *allow* Christ to come into his life. There is no other way. There are so many who are looking for a panacea to heal the sickness of the world! They look forward to some magnificent structure of conceptualized thinking which will provide the answer to everything. Or else they are looking for a "method" a "technique" which will solve all the world's problems. Ten thousand years from now there will still be those who are seeking the answers to every problem. And there will continue to be those who will stand up and ask mankind to believe that they can supply the final answer.

But there is only one *final* answer to every problem— Silence. For those who are ready, the silence will be full of meaning and they will realize that the Word of God speaks in silence. For those who are unready—only a void, an emptiness of hollow unrest until the Son of God is allowed to enter.

Some day there may be enough who have dedicated themselves to the Son of God to win mankind by the glory of their example. But down through the years it has been only a few who have loved God enough to be satisfied with His Word. The many have been led by those who have loved their own words more than *the* Word.

To what then are we called? Are we called to poverty? Yes, we are called to be poor in self that we may be rich in God. Jesus Christ did not come only to save us from death. He came that we might have life and have it more abundantly. And He showed us the way to the plenitude of being with every step that He took. For there is a fullness of comprehension given in the name of Jesus to meet each situation in life as it develops.

We do not receive the full value of His name when we limit ourselves to a stereotyped intellectualization of the riches that are in Christ.

No one can penetrate the Wisdom of God. Yet it has all been freely given—wisdom which harmonizes every situation in life—to the man or woman who receives, that is who takes it to himself. Then is there rejoicing in heaven for a space where the soul receives the essence of that which it has come upon in thought.

It has all been so freely given. We do not begin to comprehend the vastness of the blessing that has been given to all mankind. Yet each man must enter into the abiding place of truth and discover for himself that which has been so freely given.

All the work has been done for us already. Jesus Christ, through His life and victory over death upon the Cross, the same Jesus who was raised again to life—not a mere spirit, but an actual resurrection of the body—He is now Lord of all and summons us to follow His example. Nor does He ask a blind submission and a slavish imitation. He wills that each one of us should become what we *individually* are capable of becoming—an *individualized* son of God.

It is exceedingly important to realize that the Word of God is given to *each* man that comes into the world. He is "the light that enlightens every man that comes into the world." Salvation is not given en masse. It comes to every man as the free gift of God—to every man who will *accept* it as freely as it is given. Grace is not given that we may squander the gift of God in idleness. God has given us the Life that is eternal to take and use in the service of His glory. For with every gift that is divine, there is an equal responsibility for its use. Our part is to be so receptive and so attentive that we abide always in His Presence. Having done this, we cannot fail to fulfill our responsibility to God and our obligation toward mankind. In this manner we dissolve the apparent antinomy between grace and works. For grace is to no avail if we fail to *respond* to God with all our hearts and minds. Likewise all our efforts and activity are to no avail if we rely on our own strength apart from God.

Our lives should be so filled with gratitude and thanksgiving for the blessings that we receive in Christ Jesus, that we freely and spontaneously perform the works of righteousness, mercy, and humility.

With the freedom which comes with a full acceptance of the Divine Will of God given to us in Christ Jesus we find ourselves within the Kingdom of God, able to do His will because we have made His will our own. It is all so simple and natural once we accept the truth given us in the Word.

The great masters of prayer have taught us that by acceptance we can inherit all things—even the deep things of God. We do not of our own puny wills storm the citadels of prayer. We simply open the door of consciousness and allow the bliss of God to flow into our being, bringing with it the realization that "now are we the sons of God."

The Middle Ages, with all the beauty of spirit which we can find in them, did not understand the principle of acceptance sufficiently. They lived in the attitude that the planet earth itself belonged to Satan and that only within the walls of the established religion was it possible to find a foretaste of heaven. And even within the peace of the cloister the dominating conception of the body itself as a prison made it impossible for the full freedom of the Gospel to be realized. Only in Saint Francis of Assisi do we find a spirit who found in *all* of God's creation the beauty and the blessedness which He put there in the beginning.

But the bliss of God's creation, the realization of our true place in the City of God, comes to expression in consciousness only by degrees, as "the shining light, that shineth more and more unto the perfect day" (Prov. 4:18). Were we to see all things as they really are without the gradual adjustment of our vision to the light of truth, we would be blinded, bewildered, and confused—unable to use that which we would see. So we proceed by degrees to acquire that insight which makes it possible to judge all things.

As each new aspect of Divinity comes into view and we gaze upon It with single attention until we are entirely absorbed in what we behold, we are that much nearer to the Eternity for which we pray—"Thy Kingdom come" (Matt. 6:10). For God is wholly present in every part. And to behold Him in love is to behold Him in Himself.

Gradually we are transformed from small, limited, ungenerous, uncharitable creatures who seek only their own—creatures who try to piece together the broken fragments of mixed-up lives to no avail—into citizens of the Kingdom of God who see things in the clarity of simple vision.

The simplicity is so utter that we fail to comprehend it in our predilection for complexity and involvement—the simplicity of spiritual transformation. All is in the "letting." For Christ did once for us all what so many of their own accord have tried and failed to do for themselves. Just at this time in the history of the West, one finds an increasing number of those who are attempting to find a new dimension of existence by applying the disciplines of oriental religion. They are trying to force their way into the Kingdom of Reality—little realizing that all they need do is to turn around, accept Christ, and find themselves within the realm of certainty and truth.

There is that subtle pride, particularly strong in the intellectual mind, which insists upon doing everything for itself. It puts up a great show of nobleness and pretended maturity. Theirs is the loss. For the Kingdom is entered through simplicity and love and acceptance.

Furthermore the Kingdom of heaven is within us *now*, as our Lord has said. It is even more a matter of making a place for it in our hearts and minds, that the Kingdom of God may be not only a reality but a *fact* in our lives.

Christians have *now* all things that they need. For God has given the Son once for all that we may be the inheritors of His glory. It is for us to attain to the *realization* that "*now* are we the sons of God" and then to allow ourselves to be led by His spirit.

Comparatively little has been said about the doctrine of Holy Spirit. In this time, we are beginning to hear more discussion about this aspect of the Trinity than we have since the close of the Middle Ages. Particularly from Eastern Orthodoxy do we receive a considerable literature dealing with theological matters that properly relate to the doctrine of the Spirit. Nicholas Berdyaev is the most outstanding representative of this emphasis.

Christians should endeavor to listen with interest to what these representatives of the Greek tradition are trying to tell us. But it must be clearly recognized that there is a profound reason why we do not have much opinion expressed concerning the doctrine of the Holy Spirit. I submit that it may be the simple reason that the Spirit must be witnessed to rather than talked about. There is a danger that a kind of neo-Gnosticism may spring up in the West, ostensibly in the name of the Spirit, the result of which may confuse many into thinking that the imaginative speculations of some writers may be the authentic declaration of the Spirit. We are passing out of the age of rationalism and skepticism. We are in fact entering a period when men believe all sorts of things in the name of religion.

We must not be too hasty in dismissing the asseverations of Spengler simply because he committed himself to a determinist theory. Quite often, a person will perceive a trend with accuracy only to place it within a warped framework. Not only Spengler, but Keyserling and Berdyaev, each writing from entirely different presuppositions, have held the view that we are entering a period when men will grasp more deeply and inwardly the content of their respective creeds and confessions. In this sense, symbolic statements will acquire a genuine symbolic value, which value will be more widely apprehended than is now the tendency for the major portion of our society. In other words, western civilization is conceived of as entering a period of greater maturity (which Spengler likens to the period of late antiquity) wherein the values of *meaning* and *significance* will take on their due proportion in the minds of the many, or at least of the dominant minority, as Toynbee calls the creatively articulate group within a civilization. Sorokin, from a still different point of view, comes to the same general conclusion with, of course, the modifications required by his intellectual position.

The greater consciousness of depth and subtlety which these eminent men perceive in the historical trend does not mean that, in the future, humanity will necessarily be more spiritual or more Christian in the real sense of the word. It only means that Christians must become more profoundly rooted in Truth. For the possibilities of deception, distortion, and confusion in general, will be greatly multiplied as they were, comparatively speaking, in late Roman antiquity with its many varieties of Gnosticism.

Organized Christianity must, therefore, make its preparation to meet the need which is already apparent among a number of the more sensitive artistic mentalities (who usually sense the cultural trend that is beginning to emerge in their time). From this point of view, it is very likely that Augustine is much more our contemporary than John Locke or Jonathan Edwards.

There will be only one way that the false Christianity and spirituality that is gradually emerging in the historical context can be overcome, and that will be by an increasing number of Christians who will have found the Spirit of God within them. And having found the true spirit they must radiate it in all its beautiful simplicity to every person they meet and to whom they are vitally related. For organized Christianity will no longer be able to invoke the power of an emperor to crush heresy when it becomes a serious rival for membership. This instrument of control is no longer available. Particular sects may conduct heresy trials and expel the offending member. But in these times, when thought is more fluid and influence more contagious than ever before, such measures do not help much in ridding society of the confusion.

The Church, however, is secure regardless of the confusion that is sown by the opponents of Christ. For God will continue to raise up saints who will testify to His Word. They may not be canonized by men. They may live in obscurity and be of little reputation. But these are the witnesses of the Church and they shall be with us until the world is called to account.

Though these things are written, this is not to imply that the historic institution has no place in the advancement of God's decrees. But too much emphasis has been placed on the organizational aspect of religion. The world will not be made Christian by having every member of the human race belong to one organization. The ecumenical movement is not the key to the Kingdom of God.

Now the real essential Church is and remains the body of Christ of which regenerate persons are members. Therefore the Church on earth consists only of those who have been incorporated into Christ, who bow before Him, live in His Word, and adhere to His ordinances. . . .[4]

The Word of God is addressed to *each* man and each woman, alone. The *response* to the Word includes fellowship in obedience to Christ. But fellowship is not the criterion of Christianity, as some unfortunately think even at this late date.

Christians must become increasingly aware of the subtle and complicated patterns of thought which disguise themselves as expressions of Christian truth. Yet they must be able

[4] Abraham Kuyper, *Calvinism* (Grand Rapids, Mich., W. B. Eerdmans Publishing Co., 1943), p. 63.

143

to see through to the pure simplicity of the Word of God and, having seen, to abide in the vision of truth.

The world in which we now live is in process of constant change. Today one set of conditions prevails. Tomorrow there are other circumstances to contend with. Rightly we must be concerned with the whole complex of changing relationships which define our part as Christians in this world of change. Yet it is no blind change. Nor is fellowship exhausted in mutual helpfulness. When we have completed this life, we stand in a new relation to the Eternal. Then no one can point to society as his frame of reference and find his significance in the pattern of human values. Then he faces God as an individual and his possibilities for righteousness and truth have become either facts or failures.

But in eternity each shall render account as an individual. That is, eternity will demand of him that he shall have lived as an individual. Eternity will draw out before his consciousness, all that he has done as an individual, he who had forgotten himself in noisy self-conceit. In eternity, he shall be brought to account strictly as an individual, he who intended to be in the crowd where there should be no such strict reckoning. Each one shall render account to God as an individual. The King shall render account as an individual; and the most wretched beggar, as an individual. No one may pride himself at being more than an individual, and no one despondently think that he is not an individual, perhaps because here in earth's busyness he had not as much as a name, but was named after a number.[5]

[5] Sören Aabye Kierkegaard, *Purity of Heart Is to Will One Thing* (New York, Harper & Brothers, 1938), p. 169.

V

From Grace to Glory

THE concern of this book has been principally with the nature of prayer as the key to the understanding of Christianity. For Christianity is simply the term which covers the relationship between God and man through the Word of God and the Kingdom of God.

God has been so merciful to us in visiting us with His salvation that our response to Him can only be one of extreme gratitude for all that He has given us through His Word.

In this work about basic truths, the author has tried to indicate the points which need greatest clarification.

Prayer is so little understood because men have come to associate God with the idea of distance from His creation, man being thought of as of most importance in the universal scheme of things. The concept of abstract generalized man is so prevalent in the West today except among a few, that it was found necessary to show the foundations of the notion which blocks clear understanding of man's position in life. We have seen how this abstract man is a pure fiction. We realize that the Word of God addresses only individual men—

the only kind of man that exists in the eyes of God. For each individual is a special creation of God.

Man is not only to become free from the tendency which leads to disintegration but also to arrive at that most wondrous state through the love of God: namely to be called a son of God.

We have come to see that the legal concept of man is not able to contain the rich meaning of sonship. Yet it is only now that we are beginning to see more deeply into the richness of God's promise. So long as we fixed our attention mainly on the legalistic categories of guilt and acquittal, we were unable to appreciate the fullness of the love of God, who not only forgives us but draws us into a relationship with Him, a relationship which is covered by the term *son,* yet which must remain inaccessible to the mind still operating entirely within the realm of sensate values.

The reality of the Spirit so far transcends the realm of man in his fallen state that we can speak of the Spirit only in terms of faith and acceptance. Yet it is the realm of the Spirit which is promised to all who persevere till the end. And the realm of the Spirit is the Kingdom of God.

The scope of this book has been concerned with three basic aspects of the Christian religion. The whole book is simply an affirmation of the Word of God. The first part looks more directly to the *Way* by means of which we men can enter into the Kingdom of God. The second part is concerned with the necessity of perceiving and adhering to *that which is,* the truth of our existence, by cleaving through the intellectual nightmares of man-made systems. The last part of this work is essentially concerned with the acceptance of the Word in its pure simplicity, the Spirit which is life.

In the section dealing with *prayer and fasting* we looked into the basic concepts of prayer (thought of primarily as an attitude of mind) which we find represented in the teaching of Augustine, Bernard of Clairvaux and Saint John of the Cross.

The principal approach of these three men was through the application of the great principle evolved in classical thought (but deepened and enriched by a Christian content), the principle of *know thyself*. For Augustine, prayer meant the ascent of the mind and heart to God: until, gazing upon that Splendor which gives our very breath its movement and its life, we realize through the grace and truth given us in His Son—the Son of that Glory which caused the stars to shine emblazoned with His radiance—that glory and that light which shines in our hearts "to give the light of the knowledge of the glory of God in the face of Jesus Christ." How truly wondrous is that radiance and that glory! How truly infinite is the love of that most Holy God who breathes His Spirit into us and causes our hearts to move in union with His own! We are upheld and sustained by His gracious Word which feeds us with light and arouses our response— shaking loose the dust and encumbrances of this world which, through sin, has lost its way amidst the stars.

We first hear from Augustine, among the early leaders of thought within the Christian communion, how all that is human may be left behind without being destroyed when we enter into that dearest fellowship possible to man—possible not *with* man but *with God* and *to* man through God. We learn to leave behind yet not to destroy; to leave behind and yet to come back to. The human is still to be human, yet no longer bound—free to rise to Him who made us, to Him who gives us peace. Yet responsible and thus responsive to the impulse of that Love which made us and contains us, bringing into all things human the glow of charity which lights up the temple of the Living God—the most Holy Presence who lives in us when we allow our lives to take on that quickening which first came into the world with Jesus Christ. "The last Adam was made a quickening spirit" (I Cor. 15:45). To be quickened into His glory—even while on earth—and to be humbled so completely that not even a breath stirs within us but that we give thanks to Him for it; knowing with all our hearts that it is He who causes us to breathe, knowing beyond all chance of forgetting that our very lives are but dust and ashes save as we *consciously receive them from Him* who is our very Life itself.

We learn from Augustine that there is no labyrinth so deep and winding, so tortuous and filled with aching perplexity, but that the Mind of God is there—able with His infinite Intelligence to direct man on these paths which lead to peace and still more perfect peace, endlessly deeper, fuller, richer, boundlessly pure, serene, able to draw out care from every heart—able to fill all pain with radiant ecstasy entwined with light. We learn from Augustine the example of a man who is struggling with brain and heart to pierce the veil of myth, imagination, and human songs of desire and emptiness in order to seize with all his being and thus to receive the wisdom which makes us live this life more meaningfully.

Charity is born in the heart of every man who has lost the will to live in himself. Charity comes into the heart of every man who has lost the love to love in himself. Charity assumes the heart of every man who has lost the light which lights only self. Charity bears every pain, not as an effort, not as an injustice inflicted by life; but as a means to closer communion with the God in every heart—the God who first in the heart made Charity—the God, then, who still resides, though unseen, in the heart of bitterness. Charity makes this life sweet through penetration. Charity makes us grateful and receptive to the glory which our God gives to every heart that passes through the change of humility. Charity releases man from that struggling, tense pursuit of wisdom—releases and gives what is sought. Charity frees us from desire and longing and gives us love.

Charity is that point in the eternity of God where man receives the radiance of eternal Love. For man truly exists every moment in the eternity of God. But Charity is that "point" where man *knows* eternal Love and, therefore, learns what is the eternity of God. Who else can receive the knowledge of the eternal save he who first has overcome the pall of the longing which knows no bounds—that nameless thing in man whose only stirring is to stir in hunger. And man abides in hunger until he abides in Charity.

Out of his tremendous need Augustine found that faith which leads to Charity.

What then of man who finds himself again in Christ? Scripture calls him the spiritual man. And he is placed in sharp contrast with the "natural" or psychic man. Who is this natural man? He is the man whose whole existence is bound up with change—who sees every part as though it were the whole of life—who grasps at every minute as though it were a fleeting moment, not knowing that in every minute shines the glory of eternity, that the whole of life is within every part, that that change is man's cloud upon eternity—not that eternity is a static, motionless realm, but that change is the natural man's fragmentary view of Time.

In Augustine, we see the man who looks upon all things from the point of view of the Spirit. Not that he saw all things with the *eyes* of the Spirit; for he was in many ways conditioned by that which remained of the point of view of the "natural" man.

When the Spirit breaks through into our lives, there is a new beginning, a beginning from above. But this new beginning implies a way to be walked—the way of the Spirit which leads to the City of God. But the man in transit (and it is still a "natural" man in transit; the man, not the Spirit walks the way) may not see *all* with eyes of the Spirit. Jesus Christ has seen *all* with the eyes of the Spirit. We see only where we have truly walked in the Spirit. The rest is not truly seen. It is as though one were walking in the night and, at times, the light of day were to shine. When we have the light we see; when we walk in darkness we "feel" our way and carry in our consciousness the memory of what we saw in the light.

Of course, as with all analogies, this illustration cannot be applied literally. What needs to be conveyed is that the birth of the Spirit does not bring an immediate transformation of every aspect of life. But we have *begun* to see with the Spirit what we in Eternity shall see always and entirely—seeing *with* God because we shall *be* with Him as He is.

Augustine refers to the final achievement of this life as a "foretaste" of heaven. We begin to do here what we shall completely realize hereafter. In this sense, grace is the seed of glory.

Augustine also recognized the difference between the state of bondage and the state of freedom. He was the first great writer since the writing of the New Testament—and therefore he was writing as a man given grace without personal contact with the Lord or His apostles—who realized from personal experience, and wrote from that personal experience, that the locus of freedom is in the will. Without the freedom which comes with the Spirit, one is truly a slave to impulse and the conditioned judgment of his temporal existence. The psychic man is truly the servant of sin because everything he does is done with the motivation that springs from natural craving. He is either seeking pleasure or avoiding pain. The motive may be concealed from himself and the natural man may *think* that he is spiritual, but he is only deceiving himself. In the name of the finest ideals, he may be serving the very basest of motives.[1]

Therefore, since we all start in this life upon the foundation of a "natural" existence (not in the sense of having a body but with a nature which stands in need of redemption) it is only logical that the first step in preparation for that transformation, which is truly spiritual and gives us a new foundation "in the heavens," is self-knowledge that lays bare one's very motivation: the self-seeking and entirely ungodlike tendencies. When one really sees how ungodlike he is, how completely he has "lost" the likeness of God both in the sense of resemblance and in the sense of inclination, a man is in a position to see how abject his condition really is and how much he stands in need of help. When once he sees that he does not possess a single thought uncolored by a selfish, egocentric motivation, he is in a position to realize just how warped his perspective actually is. If he can face this fact and accept it as an evaluation of his actual condition as a sinner, he has by that very act become humble, truly humble—not merely self-effacing or weak as many unreflecting people conceive humility. In fact, it is only when one comes to grips with the full impact of one's "natural" condition, that one reaches out to the throne of grace. These things have nothing to do with that emotionalism which passes for religious revival in America. The latter is superficial and does not deal with the deep and hidden motivation within man. One finds this technique of thorough facing of the self (the natural

[1] One of the best studies in the subterranean life of psychic motivation is that of Hermann Alexander, Graf von Keyserling, *South American Meditations on Heaven and Hell in the Soul of Man* (New York, Harper & Brothers, 1932).

man) only in the writings of those men who, following closely in the examples set by Augustine, Bernard, and John of Yepes, have actually come to grips with that warped self, that unlikeness in the *Land of Unlikeness.*

Modern psychoanalysis is a weak caricature of the great classical tradition of the *nosce teipsum.*

I have considered it of extreme importance to draw to the attention of the Protestant world the basic principles and purposes of the mode of self-examination developed within the teachings of the great saints mentioned in this book. For Protestants have been sadly negligent in the understanding of these matters which, although only preliminary to the task of growth in grace and sanctification, must nevertheless be given their right and proper place in the building of Christian life and in the preparation for that glorious fulfillment in eternity prepared for all who wait upon the Lord in prayer and fasting (the exclusion of all unlikeness from the heart and mind).

Protestantism has too often taken a static view of the "natural" life of man. It has passed abstract theological judgments upon the condition of man in a fallen state and then has gone on to praise the new life given to man through the Word of God as though this too were something static and juridical—something which did not actually *change* the actual life of man from slavery to sin to freedom in Christ.

It is well that Protestants be reminded that for Augustine there was nothing purely formal and extrinsic about man's existence and man's hope for grace. For him it was all vital, real, and experienced as a deep and living transformation, which took him out of the bondage and compulsion to sin in which he found himself, "into the glorious liberty of the children of God" (Rom. 8:21), which is promised in Jesus Christ.

Once we have gained the humility which comes with the knowledge of what the "natural" man actually is, and we see *in ourselves* that tendency which leads away from God, we will call upon God and He shall renew us after the pattern and example, in the image and likeness of His Son, Jesus Christ.

The first part of this section treated upon the *fact* of man's existence as a state in need of redemption and regeneration.

But man has not yet come to know himself when he has discovered his unlikeness to God. He must go further. And the saints *have* gone further. For to Augustine, and all the great saints, there yet remains that in man which no sin can touch because it is that which *God Himself has conceived*, namely the *image of Himself* which is the essence and being of man. Man would not even exist as an entity without the image of God's splendor. And it is this image of Eternity at the center of man's being which is eternally with the Father. This also is our true self—the Self which our Lord said we would find when we would have lost the "self" for His sake. Our real identity, therefore, is in God; and, since it is His image who is infinite, it likewise is a partaker of infinity. When we have found God we find our true selves, our immortal identity, and we then are in truth partakers of the Divine Nature. At first we see but dimly, then gradually face to face—even as Jesus said "Blessed are the pure in heart; for they shall see God" (Matt. 5:8).

I have mentioned the name of Augustine mostly in connection with this process of self-discovery. For as was brought out in the body of this work, he set the pattern and the others developed their variations. Not that they were imitators; for each was an *individual*, a soul created by God with a unique destiny.

Jacques Maritain, whose genius is respected alike by

Catholics and Protestants, makes the following statement about Augustine, in my judgment a fine characterization:

The philosophy of which St. Augustine made use (one of the greatest religious philosophies of the world) is incontestably deficient, torn by force from the ultimate defences and spiritual fructification of dying paganism, the system of neo-Platonism. (He took it as he found it. And who is there who can read Plotinus without gratitude?) But with Augustine this philosophy is an instrument in the hands of the gift of wisdom; and no one has a clearer sense of the superiority, the heavenly transcendence of that gift, of the divine mastery with which it makes use of whatsoever instruments it will, than the great Doctor of Grace himself. What has an absolute primacy, what illuminates, discerns, commands, rules, measures, what gives a right of jurisdiction over all things, *spiritualis judicat omnia,* what exults in the breast of the christian like the waters of paradise which springs up to nourish and renew all the earth and all knowledge, is the gift of the Spirit in the power of love. A human instrument, which is certainly not mediocre, but which is imperfect, awkward and dangerous, and to direct it the most perfectly endowed hand, sensitive and holy, intelligent and wise, powerful, prudent and sagacious, the irresistible light of the superhuman Spirit—this is the admirable paradox of the wisdom of the christian Plato.[2]

We do not advocate a return to the practice and theories of the Middle Ages, either by individuals singly or in groups. But we do strongly suggest a deeper penetration into the spirit of prayer, a resource which the men discussed in the first chapter came to realize and understand. I have tried to present the essence of their understanding of prayer in such a way that the principle is readily accessible and usable to the modern mentality. And this attempt has entailed the

[2] Jacques Maritain, *The Degrees of Knowledge* (New York, Charles Scribner's Sons, 1938), pp. 362-363. Reprinted by permission.

separation of that which was purely traditional in thought and expression from that which was truly in the intent of the persons involved. We must for ourselves gain that entrance to the full understanding of the way of life which enters into Eternity.

There can be no intelligence and understanding apart from the Word of God. This injunction, which is so meaningful for every Christian, did not enter the hearts of our rationalist ancestors. They were so busy trying to prove that man was the measure of all things, and they so completely gained the attention of the dominant minority in their time, that we are still being entertained, if not bewildered, by their peculiar notions of the scheme of things.

"If any of you lack wisdom, let him ask of God, that giveth to all men liberally, and upbraideth not" (James 1:5). That is a very clear and simple statement. But it was not the kind of clarity and simplicity which men, beginning with the prominent example of Descartes, down to the present day in many cases, were seeking.

Augustine used the intellectual tools at his disposal to the extent that they could be made serviceable to the ends for which he chose to direct them. Thomas Aquinas applied himself to gain mastery of the philosophy at his disposal. And although we cannot accept many of the conclusions to which they came in their pursuit of truth, there is one thing these men of giant intellect kept steadily before them. *Their intellectual labors must harmonize with the truth of God's Word or else they were mistaken in their judgments.* Rationalists call this dogmatism, submission to blind authority, among other things. But it was much more likely *humility* of mind. Augustine succeeded more admirably than Aquinas because he more fully understood the *place* of the intellect in the order of nature. Nor was he laboring in the heat of the kind of intellectual debate in which Aquinas found himself. Hence the greater maturity and wisdom which we find in the thought of Saint Augustine.

The intelligence and understanding are set free to operate within the mind of man only when the Word of God shines His light upon the scope of our attentions. If there is no light, the attention and the rational faculty can only *feel* and upon this limited avenue of knowledge very little can be taken. But when He who is the Light of life shines in our hearts, we not only feel, we *see*. And seeing, we perceive proportion, order, relationship, perspective, color, and direction. We find the *way* of life. Finding the way, we allow our intelligence to play upon the objects of life which come to the attention until understanding is born.

The intellect that is condemned to function in a world of shadow selves and forms has very little scope, and through it only a small and distorted picture of life and truth can be acquired. But when the light of the Word is allowed to fill our minds then do we see indeed.

In the section dealing with the emergence of rationalism upon the historical scene, we tried to show the effect of the truncated perspective which the rationalistic mentality generated. The obvious conclusion which the evidence of this period thrusts upon our attention is that, far from the intelligence being "cabin'd, cribb'd, and confin'd" by a close adherence to the Word of God, it is immensely enlarged in its scope of operation because it remains in contact with life and truth. The mentality of man is narrowed and made poor by the system which threw out purpose, direction, and the presence of God from its consideration. It was not necessary to give a great deal of attention to the blunders of the seventeenth century except to call attention to the fact that the abdication of real intellectual freedom was the result of rationalism.

The proper study of mankind is God. And he who would *truly know man* must first know God. And in knowing God, he knows himself in Christ Jesus who showed us by His life in what the true likeness to God consists.

The notion of man evolved by the rationalists was truly a shattered image of the divine splendor—a mere caricature of man.

Since the seventeenth century, men have lived with this shadow foisted upon civilization—this glorification of the unlit intellect—until their view of life is so decimated and piecemeal that they wander in confusion over the face of the earth crying Light! Light! and there is no light. "God is light, and in Him is no darkness at all" (I John 1:5). Apart from Him we see nothing.

When the intelligence and understanding of men are set free through a close adherence to the Word of God, only then is it possible to speak of spiritual things. For the result will be an intelligence and understanding which is given in *wisdom* to all who *ask of God*.

It is not necessary to dwell much upon the varieties of reaction to rationalism. They are seen for what they are. All anti-intellectualism is fundamentally intellectualist.

The Spirit given by God lights up our pilgrimage on earth as we pass from eternity to eternity; and each moment, alive with meaning and purpose, is recognized within the pattern of God's boundless Intelligence, making glorious our path towards the City of God.

Christianity is Faith and Love because we must cast aside all crutches and devices we have built up in our egocentric lives, all methods and techniques figured out by the intellect of man, all athleticism and will worship which passes for spiritual discipline.

We are on our way to the City of God when once we have entered into faith, the principle of acceptance which makes it possible for the Divine Life to inform us and transform us. Life on earth is the prelude to eternity which, paradoxically, is here and now. For we do not find any sequence of change, any relative contingency and dependence in the Spirit of God. Through that little door of faith and love we enter into the Kingdom of God—or, rather, the Kingdom of God finds expression in us.

Realizing that our "natural" man remains bound up with the sequential process men call time but which really is not time (time is much more than process), we nevertheless move freely into the consciousness of our true selves when once Christ has become our life.

This beginning of true life—the life that shall have no end because it has no beginning in itself—does not lead to withdrawal from the common life of mankind. It only puts an end to that old fixated pattern of unconscious, mechanical activity which men call life but which is a mere mockery, a mere shadow-existence in a world of pungent dreams and empty longings and fears, a world of asking and receiving not, of believing only to despair. This beginning of true life establishes in the heart of the individual a center of the City of God. For the City of God is not a place with alabaster walls and golden domes; it is the living communion of all those who in this life have received again from Christ that which was lost in Adam. The end of this physical expression can mean only an unhindered continuity of life and consciousness and understanding, purified from those last vestiges of entanglement with that which the New Testament calls "psychic."

The new life, bringing with it the Way and the Truth of Christ, comes because of faith that is acceptance, and because of Love, which we accept and to which we respond.

Before Jesus Christ came into the world, there were men in every land who strove to find that which came as a free gift through Jesus Christ, the Word of God.

In the Mediterranean world, men longed for the consciousness of immortality. They developed systems of thought and worship in their attempt to find a way to life eternal. The Epistles were not written to people ignorant of these things. The literary and archeological remains of all the Mediterranean peoples show vestiges of this deep longing for a higher life than that which is bound by the sense of dimensions.

We know even more about the spiritual longings of the people of India in the age before Our Lord came to the planet earth. For here there is an unbroken continuity of tradition.

All of these religious and ascetic disciplines can be grouped together as the religions of *Eros*, the striving on the part of man after an infinite existence beyond the confines of this world of limitations. Those who lived by the law of these teachings may have gained some knowledge of Eternity. But what they gained was nevertheless a gift, although it may not have been recognized as such. For the Word has always been with mankind in every age and time. But since "the Word was made flesh, and dwelt among us" (John 1:14) we have a new relation to the Eternal. All the work of salvation has been done for us; and we who believe are the recipients of this eternal life, no more as something to be struggled for and gained through heartbreaking and extreme exertion,

159

but of a life given to each one who has faith to accept it. Yet how lightly do men hold their opportunity. They do not even know the gift of God which is for them.

No longer to strive by oneself unaided and alone—now to receive the agape which is in Christ: that is the possibility for every man.

The strange notion of a generalized abstract man with a puny intellect able to penetrate only the outer surface of things has such a hold on so many people that they do not see themselves as individuals with the potential capacity to receive the gift of sonship to God.

The Reformers, Luther and Calvin, caught the vision of the free gift of God's Word which is able to save our souls. But how many have had the faith to accept the Word of God? How many still believe that they must do everything for themselves, allowing no part in their lives for the living Word!

There are so many who fail utterly to see the simplicity of the situation in which man has been placed since the coming of the Son of God. Man has only to accept, to receive and to respond with thanksgiving and gratitude for the privilege of becoming a son of God, a living member in the true Vine whose love encompasses the heart of every living being.

The word of man must become silence. Then he will hear the Word; and, hearing, he will be able to comprehend the speech of Christ Jesus.

"Now are we the sons of God," Saint John tells us. Not tomorrow or the next day or the hour of our last breath on earth—but *now*. The Now that is God Himself, the Now of God who fills all space and speaks to us now, forever.

Now—the very essence of our existence—shapes the moments into a pattern with which we can harmonize: the Now in which God is, in which I am; the Now in which I turn and behold His Face; the Now which becomes my very life as I, with all men who value Christ above all, accept that which is given freely and without any earning on our part, the Now which is God, as love.

APPENDIX

Spirituality in Roman Catholicism

THE tradition of Saint John of the Cross has come into
great prominence in the Roman Catholic Church within
the last few decades, partly as a renewed interest in the
spiritual life of man within that communion as well as within
other sects.

Leading Catholic writers, such as Jacques Maritain and
Father Reginald Garrigou-Lagrange, have given a great
deal of attention to the possibility of associating John of the
Cross with Thomas Aquinas. Maritain, in a happy phrase,
calls Aquinas the doctor of the light and John the doctor of
the night.

While I do not go along with the Catholic interpretation
of the life and works of Saint John of the Cross, and my own
views lie distinctly outside the conception of Roman Catholicism, it is nevertheless of value to have the contrast of
the Catholic view of traditional spirituality.

The following summary is an attempt to present the
Catholic position in a fair and unprejudiced manner.

As Dom John Chapman points out in his article on Roman

Catholic mysticism,[1] the life of prayer was intensely narrowed after the reaction against spirituality in France during the latter part of the seventeenth century. The leading Spanish and French theologians, Jesuit and Dominican alike, gave little attention to the more advanced stages of prayer. Contemplation was simply the term of the meditative (discursive reasoning) process. The gifts of the Holy Ghost, the understanding of the Trinity, the Incarnation, and so forth, were listed as graces, *gratis datae,* in spite of Saint John of the Cross. Late baroque and rococo piety stressed the sensuous side of devotion, and the Spirit which we were made to behold was neglected. Instead, a tremendous increase in moral theology developed so that certain Jesuit tomes on casuistry are as legalistic as the Mishnah.

Nevertheless the past half century (following a period of aridity that lasted throughout the nineteenth century) has shown a marked increase of interest in the life of the spirit. A number of writers within the Roman tradition have written books on the spiritual life which have tended to bring the neglected heart of religion back into the sphere of the normal way of Christian development and integration.

Although Poulain, who wrote his *Graces of Interior Prayer* in 1910, still tended to make the contemplative life an extraordinary way, the more recent writers in Catholic spirituality, pre-eminently Father Garrigou-Lagrange, have "proved" that Christian perfection is based on the fulfillment of the commandment: "And thou shalt love the LORD thy God with all thine heart and with all thy soul, and with all thy might" (Deut. 6:5).

And, therefore, contemplation is in the normal way of

[1] John Chapman, "Christian, Roman Catholic Mysticism," *Encyclopaedia of Religion and Ethics,* edited by James Hastings (New York, Charles Scribner's Sons, 1951), Vol. IX, pp. 90-101.

Christian life. That is to say, perfection is a *precept* rather than a counsel.

In order to establish this claim, Father Garrigou-Lagrange (who was instrumental in having Saint John of the Cross named a Doctor of the Church in 1926), in his excellent treatise *Christian Perfection and Contemplation,* has set forth the doctrine of perfection as an integral part of moral theology. His authority is pre-eminently Saint Thomas Aquinas, who had much more to say about that branch of moral theology commonly called ascetical and mystical than is generally supposed. In addition to Saint Thomas, who supplies the doctrinal basis, the author draws on the testimony of Saint Theresa of Ávila for the practical applications, augmented by the more doctrinal writings of Saint John of the Cross and other Carmelite writers, such as Joseph of the Holy Ghost.

Saint Thomas, the prince of Catholic theologians, held to the unity of spiritual doctrine both in its theory or speculative aspect and in its practical aspect.

... moral theology, as expounded in the second part of the *Summa Theologica* of St. Thomas, keeps all its grandeur and its efficacy for the direction of souls called to the highest perfection. St. Thomas does not, in fact, consider dogmatic and moral theology as two distinct sciences; sacred doctrine, in his opinion, is absolutely one and is of such high perfection that it contains the perfections of both dogmatic and moral theology. In other words, it is eminently speculative and practical, as the science of God from which it springs. That is why he treats in detail in the moral part of his *Summa* not only human acts, precepts, and counsels, but also habitual and actual grace, the infused virtues in general and in particular. The gifts of the Holy Ghost, their fruits, the beatitudes, the active and contemplative life, the degrees of contemplation, graces gratuitously bestowed, such as the gift of miracles, the gift of tongues, prophesy, and rapture, and likewise the religious life and its various forms. ...

Appendix

The cycle formed by the different parts of theology, with its evident unity, is thus completed. Sacred science proceeds from revelation contained in Scripture and Tradition, preserved and explained by the teaching authority of the church. It arranges in order all revealed truths and their consequences in a single doctrinal body, in which the precepts and counsels are set forth as founded on the supernatural mystery of the divine life, of which grace is a participation. Lastly, it shows how, by the practice of the virtues and docility to the Holy Ghost, the soul not only arrives at belief in the revealed mysteries, but also at the enjoyment of them and at a grasp of the profound meaning of the word of God, source of all supernatural knowledge, and at a life of continual unity with the Blessed Trinity who dwells in us. Doctrinal mysticism thus appears as the final crown of all acquired theological knowledge, and it can direct souls in the way of experimental mysticism. *This latter is an entirely supernatural and infused loving knowledge* [italics mine], full of sweetness, which only the Holy Ghost, by His action, can give us and which is, as it were, the prelude of the beatific vision. Such is manifestly the conception of ascetical and mystical theology which has been formulated by the great masters of sacred science, especially by St. Thomas Aquinas.[2]

From the above quotations, there can be no question left as to the vital part played by spiritual doctrine in the unity of dogma.

Once it is established that mystical theology is an integral part of sacred science, the question of its significance and value arises. Particularly in modern times, one is confronted with this question; not in the terms expressed here, but as a contrast, almost contradiction, to the practical, empirical approach which confines itself to the description of phenomenal states and the practical means of inducing them.

[2] Reginald Garrigou-Lagrange, O.P., *Christian Perfection and Contemplation* (London, B. Herder, 1937), pp. 13-14. This and subsequent quotations are reprinted by permission.

The latter method of approach ends logically in psychology. It is evidently subjective in its appreciation; and, since it does not distinguish among the gifts of the Holy Ghost, one of which is infused contemplation, it tends to lump together extraordinary phenomena with the normal signs of spiritual development. The result is that the whole aspect of the spiritual life is divorced from the context of normal Christian experience and relegated to the domain of extraordinary graces which are arbitrarily conferred upon the soul without preparation. The natural consequence of this attitude is a discouragement of interest in what Garrigou-Lagrange calls the normal way of sanctity. Evidence of this sad state is found in the narrowing of the Christian way to an avoidance of sin and a moral adherence to the virtues available to the natural man. Also the tools of psychology, by means of which the greater is measured by the lesser, are used to pass judgment upon the life of the spirit with its transformation of the individual soul. Let the psychologist become a saint and he will be in a better position to *understand* the laws of the spiritual life. Father Garrigou-Lagrange assumes the inseparableness of the speculative and the practical in approaching the problem of Christian perfection.

Ascetical and mystical theology is the application of theology in the direction of souls toward an ever more intimate union with God. It must use the inductive and deductive methods, studying the facts of the spiritual life in the light of revealed principles and of the theological doctrines deduced from these principles.[3]

Before analyzing the distinction and relation between the ascetical and mystical aspects, it would be well to cite the author's views on the causes for the neglect of the spiritual life. Molinism was only one contributing factor. The formal

[3] *Ibid.*, p. 23.

result of the narrowed scope of Christian life was the separation of the ascetical from the mystical theology.

This division followed upon lively discussions that were occasioned by abuse springing from a premature and erroneous teaching of the mystical ways. From the time of St. Teresa, these ways seem to many theologians so suspect that the writings of St. John of the Cross had to be defended against the charge of Manicheism, and superiors were aroused to the point of forbidding their religious to read the works of Venerable John Tauler, Ruysbroek, Blessed Henry Suso, St. Gertrude, and St. Mechtildis. After the condemnation of the errors of Molinos, the mystical ways were even more suspect.

Since then a rather large number of authors, who are excellent in many respects, have agreed on making an absolute distinction between ascetical and mystical theology. Excessively eager to systematize things and to establish a doctrine to remedy abuses, and consequently led to classify things materially and objectively, without a sufficient lofty and profound knowledge of them, they declare that ascetical theology should treat of the "ordinary" Christian life according to the three ways, the purgative, the illuminative, and the unitive. As for mystical theology, it should treat only of extraordinary graces, among which they include not only visions and private revelations, but also supernatural, confirmed contemplation, the passive purifications, and the mystical unity.

Therefore the mystical union no longer appears in their arrangement as the activating point of the normal development of sanctifying grace, of the virtues, and of the gifts. According to their view, infused contemplation is not the life of faith and the spirit of wisdom carried to their perfection, to their full efflorescence; but it seems rather to be attached to graces *gratis datae*, such as prophecy, or at least to an entirely extraordinary or miraculous mode of the gifts of the Holy Ghost. Because they place the mystical union and infused contemplation among the graces *gratis datae*, these authors counsel already fervent souls against seeking not only visions and private revelations, but also the mystical union and infused contemplation, if they would avoid all presumption and advance in humility: *altiori te ne quaesieris*. This seems quite like the mistake made by those spiritual directors who refused daily communion to these same souls, alleging that humility does not permit one to aim so high.[4]

Traditionally the whole of the Christian way of life has been considered in such a way that the contemplative stage was seen in organic unity with the active life.

St. Thomas especially showed the relation between what are today called ascetical theology and mystical theology, by treating of the mutual relations of action and contemplation. With St. Augustine and St. Gregory, this is what he teaches: the active life, to which is attached the exercise of the moral virtues of prudence, justice, fortitude, and temperance, and the outward works of charity, prepare for the contemplative life, in so far as it regulates the passions which disturb contemplation, and in so far as it makes us grow in the love of God and of our neighbor. Then the contemplation of God, which is proper to the perfect, leads to action, directs it, and renders it much more supernatural and fruitful. Thus in the natural order the image precedes the idea and then serves to express it; the emotion precedes the will and then serves to execute with greater ardor the thing willed; and so again, says St. Thomas, our acts engender a habit, then this habit makes us act more promptly and easily. In this way asceticism does not cease when the contemplative life begins; on the contrary, the exercise of the different virtues becomes truly superior when the soul receives the mystical grace of a continual union with God.[5]

Since the integrity of the Christian life is to be upheld against all efforts to truncate the spiritual aspect of our existence, wherein constitutes the essential nature of the

[4] *Ibid.*, pp. 27-28.
[5] *Ibid.*, p. 25.

mystical life? As the term is used in this treatise by Garrigou-Lagrange, it signifies the stage of life in which there is a predominance of the gifts of the Holy Ghost over the virtues of the ascetical life.

Ascetical theology ... treats of the Christian life of beginners, and of those who advance with the help of grace in the exercise of the Christian virtues, the mode of which remains a human mode adapted to that of our faculties. On the other hand, mystical theology treats especially of the unitive life of the perfect, in which there is clearly manifest the divine mode of the gifts of the Holy Ghost, in the exercise of which the soul is more passive than active, and in which it obtains a "quasi-experimental" knowledge of God present in it, as St. Thomas explains.[6]

"Men ought always to pray, and not to faint" (Luke 18:1), is a statement of Jesus which applies to all Christians, though only those who have been made perfect through agape will fulfill this precept entirely.

The term *ascetical life* refers simply to that phase of Christian growth in which prayer is essentially active, that is, the human mode predominates. The term *mystical life* refers to that phase of Christian growth in which the divine mode prevails. It is the Holy Ghost which prays in us from this point on. The spirit cries within us, *Abba* (father). Contemplation is "infused"; this means simply that stillness having been acquired by the soul, the Holy Ghost can bear witness to the Father and the Son, leading us into all truth. This speaking and hearing is entirely supernatural in mode. It has nothing to do with auditions, visions, rapture, ecstasy and other phenomena which all the masters of the spiritual life have agreed to label extraordinary, having no relation at all to the life of sanctifying grace.

[6] *Ibid.*, p. 33.

Appendix

Having clarified certain basic terms applied to the Christian life which consists essentially in the way of perfection, it remains necessary only to identify the essence of perfection and the end for which we were made.

Saint Thomas says, "A thing is said to be perfect in so far as it attains its proper end, which is the ultimate perfection thereof." Hence perfection does not consist in the virtues as the means in relation to the end, which for man is union with God. Now God is love and as Saint John tells us that he that abideth in love abideth in God and God abideth in him. Also St. Paul says that Charity is the bond of perfection. Faith and hope are swallowed up in glory when we behold the divine essence and know even as we are known; but Charity, the love of God in us, will remain forever. Hence the essence of perfection is Charity which principally unites us to God, who is Love. "On these two commandments hang all the law and the prophets" (Matt. 22:40).

The increase of charity proportionately increases our receptivity to the gift of divine wisdom which gives us an understanding of the mysteries of faith.

The end to which perfection tends is consummated in glory, of which grace is the seed. Father Garrigou-Lagrange in a moving passage describes the life of the blessed in heaven thus:

... they enter heaven in the cycle of the Blessed Trinity who dwells in them. The Father engenders His Word in them; the Father and the Son breathe forth love in them. Charity likens them to the Holy Ghost; the beatific vision makes them like the Word, who renders them like the Father of Whom He is the image. In each of them the Trinity, known and loved, dwells as in a living tabernacle; and furthermore, they are in the Trinity, at the summit of being, of thought, and of love.[7]

[7] *Ibid.*, p. 120.

Appendix

In conclusion, it is well to indicate that by no means all Catholics accept the analysis of the contemplative life as Father Garrigou-Lagrange, a leading Thomist, has presented it. Notable among the dissenters is Father Gabriel of Saint Mary Magdalen who, as professor of Spiritual Theology in the International College of Saint Teresa of the Discalced Carmelites, Rome, is qualified to give a criticism which can be respectfully pondered.

A large part of his book, *St. John of the Cross, Doctor of Divine Love and Contemplation,* is devoted to the differences between the Thomists and Carmelites on the subject of "acquired" contemplation. This subtle, but extremely important stage of the contemplative life, has not yet been studied or mutually decided upon by all the theologians of the present.